COLLECTION GALÉE

GALÉE

BTS
TERTIAIRES

ANGLAIS

BTS 1re année

Nouvelle édition

Anne Bellenger
Claude Renucci

Nathan
TECHNIQUE

Crédit photographique

p. 71 : Olivier Roque ; p. 84 : Ken Goff Photos, SIPA ; p. 156 : DR/SAFEWAY.

Coordination éditoriale : Christine Asin
Édition : Virginie Legrand/Sylvie Ogée/Gaël Gauvin
Coordination artistique : Evelyn Audureau
Conception maquette : Fiat Lux
Composition : CGI
Iconographie : Véronique Brown
Illustration : François Dimberton
Cartes : Séraph
Fabrication : Françoise Leroy

ISBN : 978-2-09-160358-2

Sommaire

Texts & Practice

Background & Activities

▶▶▶

Présentation de l'ouvrage

Vous entrez en classes post-baccalauréat. Votre objectif est de consolider ce que vous avez appris au lycée en anglais et de compléter ces acquis par des compétences particulières à votre section (lexique et idées).

Les examens post-bac prennent la forme d'un oral, d'un écrit ou des deux.

Vous devez montrer que vous avez compris un document : cette compréhension peut être un compte rendu structuré, un résumé, une traduction en français, etc. Vous devrez aussi faire la preuve que vous êtes capable de vous exprimer en anglais : oralement ou par écrit (compte rendu ou résumé d'un document, lettre, réponses à des questions, présentation, etc.).

Cet ouvrage a pour objectif de vous aider à acquérir les connaissances de base et la méthodologie nécessaires.

Il propose un travail sur six thèmes fondamentaux (entreprises, travail, consommateurs, distribution, environnement et nouvelles technologies), et est organisé en trois blocs :

1. Texts & Practice

Pour chacun des six thèmes abordés, vous disposez de huit documents variés, authentiques et récents :

- Trois textes accompagnés de questions organisées selon la démarche suivante :

• ***première partie :*** repérage de compréhension. Des questions en français ou en anglais vous permettent de vérifier que vous avez repéré les éléments essentiels du document ;

• ***deuxième partie :*** repérage de langue sur le document : recherche lexicale, manipulations de chiffres, rappels et exercices sur des points essentiels de grammaire ;

• ***troisième partie :*** acquisition de méthodes (faire une introduction, répondre aux questions en *Wh-* pour aboutir à un compte rendu, conclure, écrire une lettre, traduire, faire des recherches sur Internet, participer à un jeu de rôle, etc.) ;

- Quatre textes complémentaires pour vous entraîner à l'oral ou à l'écrit en appliquant les méthodes suggérées ;

- Un texte en français accompagné de questions pour l'exploiter en anglais.

La totalité des articles en anglais est enregistrée sur le CD audio.

▶▶▶

2. Background & Activities

Background : des connaissances indispensables sur la vie socio-économique. Traité de manière simple et claire, accompagné d'un lexique anglais-français sur la même page, ce cours vous permet de mettre les articles proposés en perspective.

Activities : des exercices vous permettent de vérifier la bonne acquisition des connaissances (phrases de thème, textes à trous, questions, graphiques, etc.).

3. Survival kit ...

Il regroupe, sous forme de fiches :

- des conseils de méthode pour aborder les différents exercices oraux et écrits ;
- des éléments indispensables de lexique (chiffres, graphiques) ;
- des cartes de la Grande-Bretagne, des États-Unis, de l'Europe, de l'Inde et de la Chine.

Chapter 1. Firms

Document 1

A new look for Ronald McDonald

Ronald McDonald, the iconic mascot clown of fast food giant McDonald's since 1963, is to be given a new sporty look.

Traditionally famous for its red hair and yellow jump suit, the clown will be seen kicking a football and snowboarding with a basketball star in a TV commercial to be screened next week.

Hopefully, the leaner, more health-conscious Ronald, whose official title within the company is "chief happiness officer", will encourage children to get up on their feet and start moving at a time when obesity is becoming a growing health issue in many countries.

Images of hamburgers and fries, the food McDonald's is best known for, will be absent from the campaign.

Officials said this commercial was part of their new message about food as McDonald's, which operates 30,000 restaurants worldwide, has been criticized for its foods being unhealthy and fattening.

The company has also revamped its menus. It now sells salads and fruit alongside with hamburgers, fries and milkshakes.

ITV News online, May 23, 2006.

Looking for words

a. à statut d'icône : ……………

b. combinaison : ……………

c. taper dans : ……………

d. spot publicitaire : ……………

e. diffuser : ……………

f. aminci : ……………

g. santé : ……………

h. problème : ……………

i. exploiter : ……………

j. frites : ……………

k. dans le monde entier : ……………

……………

l. qui fait grossir : ……………

m. remanier : ……………

Figures

Survival kit, p. 183

Écoutez, écrivez et lisez à haute voix les chiffres que vous repérez.

a. Deux dates.
Que remarquez-vous pour les années après l'an 2000 ? Quelle est la différence avec les années qui précèdent l'an 2000 ?

……………

……………

b. Un nombre : ……………

c. Que peut-on dire du mot *thousand* ?

……………

d. Une date : ……………

e. Dites-la à haute voix. Qu'avez-vous rajouté ?

……………

f. Comment peut-on aussi écrire cette date ?

……………

g. Comment diriez-vous les dates suivantes : *21 April* ? *24 June* ? *25 August* ?

……………

Document 1 Practice

PREMIÈRE PARTIE : REPÉRAGE DE COMPRÉHENSION

❶ Exprimez l'idée générale de ce document en français

❷ Analysez le titre et le premier paragraphe (l. 1 à 4)

Survival kit, p. 167

a. Repérez le nom propre dans le titre.
b. Qu'apporte le premier paragraphe par rapport au titre ?

❸ Repérez dans le texte

a. Le nom de l'entreprise.
b. Son secteur d'activité.
c. Sa taille.
d. Le nom du clown mascotte de l'entreprise.
e. Sa tenue fétiche.
f. Son titre officiel.
g. Ce qui va changer dans son nouvel aspect.
h. Un menu traditionnel chez McDonald's.
i. Un menu « nouveau » chez McDonald's.

❹ Vérifiez que vous avez compris

a. Depuis quelle date Ronald McDonald est-il la mascotte de l'entreprise ?
b. Que va faire Ronald McDonald dans le nouveau spot publicitaire ?
c. Quel est l'objectif du message ?
d. Pourquoi l'entreprise McDonald's diffuse-t-elle un tel spot ?
e. Quels types d'aliments seront absents de la publicité ?

DEUXIÈME PARTIE : REPÉRAGE DE LANGUE

❶ La reformulation

Reformulez les phrases suivantes en utilisant pour les mots soulignés des synonymes trouvés dans l'article.

a. Ronald McDonald is the mascot of <u>the huge company specialized in fast food</u> McDonald's.

....

....

b. The new <u>TV ad</u>, with a <u>thinner</u> Ronald, <u>will be broadcast</u> next week.

....

c. Images of hamburgers and fries, the food McDonalds is <u>famous for</u>, <u>will not be seen</u>.

....

....

d. Critics say that McDonald's food is <u>not good for you</u> because it <u>makes you fat</u>.

....

....

e. McDonald's has also <u>modified</u> its menus.

....

❷ L'expression du futur

a. L'article présente un nouveau spot télévisé de l'entreprise McDonald's qui va passer « la semaine prochaine ». Les verbes expriment donc une idée de futur. Relevez-les.

– L. 3-4 : The clown .... a new look.

– L. 7 : The clown .... kicking a ball.

– L. 15-16 : Ronald .... children.

– L. 23 : Images of hamburgers and fries .... from the campaign.

b. Comment peut-on exprimer une idée au futur ? Connaissez-vous d'autres formes verbales ?

....

....

❸ Poser des questions

a. Transformez les phrases suivantes par des questions auxquelles on répondra par « oui » ou par « non ».

– McDonald's operates 30,000 restaurants worldwide.

....

– McDonald's now sells salads because it is healthier.

....

– The commercial will be screened on TV next week.

....

b. Que remarquez-vous concernant l'ordre des mots ?

....

❹ Traduction en anglais

a. L'entreprise McDonald's est critiquée parce que ses menus font grossir et ne sont pas bons pour la santé.

....

b. Dans le nouveau spot publicitaire, on va voir le clown taper dans un ballon.

....

TROISIÈME PARTIE : ACQUISITIONS DE MÉTHODES

❶ Entraînez-vous au compte rendu oral en anglais

▶ **Survival kit**, p. 171

a. Préparez l'introduction (source, idée générale du document) en répondant aux questions en *Wh-*.

b. Faites un plan du texte.
1. Facts concerning McDonald's and Ronald McDonald
2. Problems
3. The company's reaction

c. Préparez la conclusion.

❷ Branching out

a. In what way does McDonald's follow the 5Ps of the marketing mix?

b. What else could the company do to increase its profits?

Document 2

Problems for the Big Three automakers

The Ford Motor Company said on Monday that it would close as many as 14 factories and cut up to 30,000 jobs in North America by 2012, to fight against foreign competitors who have taken more than 40% of the American market.

The move by Ford, the second largest automaker in the USA, comes two months after General Motors, the industry leader said it would close all or part of a dozen factories and eliminate a similar number of jobs.

Including cuts that took place at the Chrysler Corporation, the Big Three automakers have eliminated or announced plans to axe nearly 140,000 jobs since 2000, about a third of their North American payroll.

But the US automakers' restructuring plans do not mean the end of car manufacturing in the USA. The geographic localisation of the factories is moving south, where a new auto industry is booming.

Japanese, German and South Korean companies now employ 60,000 people, a younger, cheaper workforce with lower wages and fewer benefits than the Detroit workers were getting.

And those foreign companies are expanding their factories. Later this year, Toyota will open a new truck plant in San Antonio.

The Detroit Post,
25 February 2006.

up to: jusqu'à
competitor: concurrent
to axe: supprimer
payroll: masse salariale
to boom: prospérer
workforce: main-d'œuvre
wage: salaire
benefit: avantage social
truck: camion

Document 3

Chinese workers rebel over conditions

Last Monday, four major American companies, Walt Disney, Mattel, Hasbro and McDonald's ordered an investigation into allegations that a riot had erupted at a big toy supplier in the Chinese city of Dongguan.

Executives at the company said there was increasing evidence that the workers were beginning to resent the long hours, low pay and poor working environments in the factories of the Guangdong Province, which borders Hong Kong.

Millions of production workers from all over China have found jobs in the region in the hope of escaping the poverty of the country's remote inland regions.

The Guangdong factories have become the engine of China's booming export industry, as the huge pool of low-cost labour has allowed manufacturers to cut production costs.

McDonald's and Disney representatives in Hong Kong expressed concern on Monday and said the suppliers were required to follow long-established codes of conduct governing the working conditions. All the companies said labour audits were regularly carried out to be sure suppliers respected minimum labour standards, fair terms of employment, safe and clean environments.

The Washington Journal,
9 August 2006.

investigation: enquête
riot: émeute
supplier: fournisseur
executive: cadre
to resent: ne pas aimer
to escape: fuir, échapper à
remote: lointain
inland: de l'intérieur
engine: moteur
safe: sans danger

Présentez ces deux textes à l'oral.

Survival kit, p. 171

Document 4

Zara gives style to the public

Launched by the reclusive businessman Amancio Ortega from his sister-in-law's kitchen table in A Coruna*, the chic clothing chain has boomed so spectacularly that even snootier Spanish competitors acknowledge it has educated a nation's dress sense and revolutionised the wardrobe of a generation. [...]

Zara is the mightiest arm of Mr Ortega's Inditex textile empire, whose phenomenal growth has made its founder Spain's wealthiest man. [...]

The company is valued at around 9.3bn euros, putting it up there with Gap, Benetton and H&M, and 52 per cent of sales are generated from stores in 33 countries outside Spain. [...]

The rate of growth in recent years has been "intense" as the latest annual report puts it. Net income rose last year by 27 per cent, net revenues by 28 per cent.

Zara has never conducted an advertising campaign. Word of mouth, and the rapidly changing clothes on offer, seem magnetic enough for customers to come flocking through the doors. The company owes its success to swiftly identifying stylish catwalk trends and bringing them to the high street at a fraction of the cost, within days.

Despite its international span, 80 per cent of Zara's clothes are made in Europe, overwhelmingly at its hi-tech factories in Arteixo. The company has invested heavily in the latest machines for cutting and dyeing, and assembly is handled by smaller factories nearby. The entire operation is computerized so popular lines in all shops can be boosted and flagging ones whipped away, or replaced by more popular versions, in less than two weeks. [...]

The philosophy behind Zara was established in the early Sixties [...].

"Last year [1999] marked the 25th anniversary of the group's first store," Mr Ortega writes in the annual report, the nearest he gets to a public statement. "A lot has changed, from the world we live in to the company itself. But one thing hasn't changed, the innovative spirit that was the driving force back then. Today we number 24,000 professionals worldwide, who each day tackle the same goal that we set when we opened that first store: to satisfy the needs of our customers with the latest in fashion."

Elisabeth Nash, *The Independent*, 23 May 2001.

*A Coruna = La Corogne : ville de Galice (nord-ouest de l'Espagne), siège du groupe Inditex.

reclusive: solitaire
snooty: arrogant
mighty: puissant
arm: (ici) branche
catwalk: passerelle de défilé de mode
to flag: baisser
to whip away: retirer

Zara in 2006: 2,700 stores in 80 countries – 5M€ turnover in 2005 – 13 factories – 60% of sales overseas – 3,000 employees in Spain.

Looking for words

a. lancer (une entreprise) : ....
b. concurrent : ....
c. ventes : ....
d. magasins (2 mots) : ....
e. taux de croissance : ....
f. rapport annuel : ....
g. revenu (2 mots) : ....
h. campagne de pub : ....
i. bouche-à-oreille : ....
j. se presser : ....
k. tendance : ....
l. centre-ville : ....
m. envergure : ....
n. usine : ....
o. informatisé : ....
p. entreprise : ....
q. teindre : ....
r. montage : ....
s. augmenter : ....
t. déclaration publique : ....
....
u. s'attaquer à : ....

Document 4 **Practice**

PREMIÈRE PARTIE : REPÉRAGE DE COMPRÉHENSION

❶ Exprimez l'idée générale de ce document en français

❷ Analysez le titre et le premier paragraphe (l. 1 à 10)

Survival kit, p. 167

a. Repérez les noms propres dans le titre et dans le premier paragraphe.
b. Quel mot du titre indique de quel secteur d'activité il s'agit ?
c. Quels mots du premier paragraphe reprennent la même idée ?
d. Quelle est la nationalité de l'entreprise ?

❸ Repérez dans le texte

a. L'implantation géographique de l'entreprise (siège et usines).
b. Le nom de son fondateur.
c. Le nom du groupe.
d. La date de sa fondation.
e. Le nombre de salariés.

❹ Vérifiez que vous avez compris

a. Où sont vendus la majorité des produits de l'entreprise ?
b. Quel est le pourcentage de ses ventes à l'export ?
c. Qui sont ses concurrents ?

DEUXIÈME PARTIE : REPÉRAGE DE LANGUE

❶ Les chiffres

Survival kit, p. 184

a. Écrivez en chiffres : *The early sixties.*

....

b. Comment diriez-vous :

– le milieu des années 1960 ? ....

– la fin des années 1960 ? ....

c. Complétez les phrases suivantes avec des chiffres du texte et lisez-les à haute voix.

– The article was published on .... May .... in *The Independent*.

– In .... the Inditex group celebrated its .... anniversary.

– The company numbers .... professionals worldwide.

– .... of Zara's clothes are made in Europe.

– The company is valued at around .... euros.

– .... of sales are generated in .... countries outside Spain.

d. Écrivez en toutes lettres les chiffres obtenus dans l'exercice précédent.

– ....

– ....

– ....

– ....

– ....

– ....

❷ La reformulation

Reformulez les phrases suivantes avec des expressions du texte.

- L. 24-25 : The company's revenues skyrocketed last year.

....

- L. 33 : It is successful because...

....

- L. 45-46 : Local subcontractors assemble the parts.

....

❸ L'emploi des formes verbales

a. Relevez dans le quatrième paragraphe (l. 22 à 26) :

- une phrase au *present perfect* : ....

....

- une phrase au prétérit : ....

....

b. Justifiez l'emploi de ces deux formes verbales.

....

....

c. Retrouvez dans l'article trois phrases au *present perfect* qui expriment des bilans.

– ....

– ....

– ....

d. Retrouvez dans l'article deux phrases au prétérit qui expriment un passé daté.

– ....

– ....

e. Complétez les phrases suivantes en utilisant le prétérit ou le *present perfect* et en conjuguant le verbe indiqué entre parenthèses.

- Amancio Ortega .... Zara, a group specialized in fashion retailing, in 1974. (create)

- His company .... now .... the Inditex group. (become)

- The Inditex group, now quoted on the Stock Exchange, ... with several fashion retail chains: Zara, Pull & Bear, Massimo Dutti, Bershka and Stradivarius. (develop)

- In the annual report, the Chairman says: "A lot .... since we .... our philosophy in the early sixties." (change – establish)

- The rate of expansion .... high in 2000, with 158 new stores in Europe, America and Asia. (be)

❹ La forme passive

a. Les phrases ci-dessous sont à la forme passive : soulignez la forme verbale.

- (The company) was launched by Amancio Ortega – the firm is located in Galicia.
- The company is valued at 9.3bn euros – 52% of the sales are generated from...
- 80% of Zara's clothes are made in Europe – Assembly is handled by small factories – Popular articles can be boosted or replaced in less than two weeks.
- The philosophy was established in the early Sixties.

b. Relevez ci-dessus les deux phrases qui comportent un complément d'agent, soulignez-le et expliquez sa présence.

– ....

....

– ....

....

c. Pourquoi les autres phrases à la forme passive ci-dessus n'ont-elles pas de complément d'agent ?

....

❺ Les noms composés : l'ordre des mots

a. Retrouvez, dans le premier paragraphe (l. 1 à 10) du document, une expression qui désigne l'entreprise (son secteur) et qui la caractérise.

....

b. Observez.

> **– En français, l'ordre des mots est inversé (« une entreprise de confection à la mode »).**
> **– En anglais, on place le plus près du nom (qui se trouve à la fin) ce qui est le plus important : le secteur, puis le reste.**
> **Notez qu'en français, la phrase est longue et peut comporter des propositions relatives, alors qu'elle est beaucoup plus compacte en anglais.**

c. Traduisez en français les expressions suivantes.

- A profitable American fastfood chain: ....

....

- The innovative Spanish fashion designers: ....

....

d. Traduisez en anglais les expressions suivantes :

- Le gros fabricant de fromage hollandais : ....

....

- Le joueur de tennis français dont on parle : ....

....

❻ Les comparatifs de supériorité

a. Relevez dans le texte trois adjectifs au comparatif de supériorité.

....

b. Écrivez les adjectifs à la forme simple.

....

c. Expliquez la différence de construction pour les adjectifs longs et courts.

....

❼ Les superlatifs

a. Relevez dans le texte quatre superlatifs.

....

b. Écrivez les trois adjectifs et l'adverbe à la forme simple.

....

❽ Traduction en anglais

a. Beaucoup de choses ont changé depuis 1974, mais une chose n'a pas changé : notre esprit d'innovation pour satisfaire les besoins de nos clients.

....

....

b. 80 % des vêtements vendus par le groupe Inditex sont fabriqués en Galice, alors que les concurrents délocalisent la production dans des pays à bas salaires.

....

....

c. Le groupe a ouvert 158 magasins l'an dernier.

....

d. Les clients aiment acheter la dernière mode chez Zara.

....

TROISIÈME PARTIE : ACQUISITION DE MÉTHODES

❶ Rédigez un compte rendu en anglais

▶ Survival kit, p. 173

a. Introduction (source, idée générale du document) en répondant aux questions en *Wh-* en une phrase.

b. Plan
1. The company
2. The reasons for its success

c. Conclusion

❷ Présentez en français

▶ Survival kit, p. 173

Votre objectif est de rédiger une présentation structurée des différentes composantes du succès de Zara. Cette présentation devra comporter 120 mots (+/– 10 %).

a. Repérez les éléments demandés.

b. Présentez ces idées de manière structurée.

❸ Traduisez le paragraphe 5 (l. 27 à 37) en français

▶ Survival kit, p. 174

❹ Branching out

▶ Survival kit, pp. 180, 176, 177

a. Trouvez des informations sur Internet sur l'entreprise (www.inditex.com) et faites une présentation en anglais qui complète l'étude de l'article.

b. Préparez votre curriculum vitæ et une lettre de motivation en vue d'un stage dans le groupe Inditex.

1

Document 5

How Vanessa went global with her job

Vanessa and David Phillips were a successful couple in London with careers in banking. When children came along – the couple have twin sons aged 11 and a seven-year-old daughter – the family moved to King's Lynn in Norfolk for an improved quality of life. Vanessa, who had been a secretary before going into banking, knew a couple of clients who wanted typing done.

Working from home suited her, but there were problems. Vanessa explains: "We had to rely on tapes being sent backwards and forwards in the post and inevitably, there were delays. What changed everything was the onset of broadband telephony."

Today, Vanessa runs a thriving business, Outsec, employing herself, her husband, four heads of department and more than 80 secretaries working from their homes in countries around the world. Vanessa's business started expanding when she realized that she had more work than she could cope with, and advertised in her local paper for additional help. "The secretaries in the business today don't have to be local," she says. "Thanks to the internet, they can be anywhere across the globe. We have people working from home in New Zealand, America, and mainland Europe. What matters is not the location but the quality of their work."

The secretaries, who are paid by monthly invoices, all have experience in the sectors in which Outsec specializes: surveying, estate agency, accountancy, legal, medico-legal, and medical. All are sectors in which practitioners need lengthy reports typed up and where e-mails are not appropriate.

Every secretary is allocated his or her own client. "That way," says Vanessa, "there is a one-to-one relationship and the secretary can get inside the head of the client."

The business is still run from Vanessa's home, although its growth may force a move. But it is fundamental to Outsec that its secretaries can work from their homes. She says that many of them have family commitments, "so this is ideal for them."

The Times, October 12, 2005.

to rely on: dépendre de
tape: enregistrement
delay: retard
broadband: haut débit
thriving: prospère
to cope with: faire face à
invoice: note de frais
surveying: expertise topographique
estate agency: agence immobilière
accountancy: comptabilité
practitioner: (ici) professionnel
commitments: responsabilités

Faites un compte rendu oral de ce texte en anglais.

Survival kit, p. 171

Document 6

All the rage since Reagan

Nike's Air Force 1, introduced in the early 1980s, still grabs attention – and huge margins.

Once the word hits the street, hundreds of teens start lining up at stores. So strong is demand that new releases happen only at weekends – so kids won't skip school. When the doors open, they sell out in hours. Tickets for the current Eminem tour? the new iPod music player? Nope. We're talking about a basic basketball sneaker, Nike Inc's Air Force 1.

Launched in 1982, when Ronald Reagan was in the White House, the sneaker is almost pathetically low-tech. Yet the Air Force 1 remains the definition of urban cool.

In 25 years, AF1 racked up an estimated $1 billion in sales and generated profit margins of 70%, say analysts – double that of other sneakers.

How do you keep a basic sneaker hot for a quarter-century? Nike's genius is that it has managed to market a classic without alienating teens. At the same time, Nike creates consumer longing by keeping supplies tight and releasing collectible versions with minimal hype.

AF1 advertising is minimal today. Mostly, Nike lets the customers – and the rappers – do the talking. And such is the shoe's cult status that teenagers hang out at NikeTalk.com and other chat rooms to find out when the next AF1 is coming.

Every two months or so, Nike releases a new shoe. Each release involves roughly 350,000 to 500,000 pairs of shoes shipped nationwide, and each store gets about 25 to 30.

The Air Force 1 is a Nike profit machine. The company sells each pair to retailers for about $48,50 but pays just $12 to make them in Asia.

Since the design has remained essentially unchanged, there are few developments costs, and of course Nike no longer pays anyone to promote them.

Adapted from *Business Week*, July 25, 2005.

---

teen (= teenager): adolescent
sneaker: chaussure de sport

Looking for words

a. attirer : ....

b. énorme : ....

c. marge : ....

d. faire la queue : ....

e. sortie : ....

f. manquer : ....

g. lancer : ....

h. basique : ....

i. élégant/branché (2 mots) : ....

j. rapporter : ....

k. bénéfice : ....

l. désir : ....

m. approvisionnement : ....

n. publicité (2 mots) : ....

o. traîner : ....

p. détaillant : ....

Document 6 **Practice**

PART 1: UNDERSTANDING THE TEXT

1 Give the general idea of the article

2 Analyse the title and the subtitle

a. Is the title explicit?
b. Answer *Wh-* questions in the subtitle.

3 Find the following information in the article

a. The name of the company.
b. The name of the shoe.
c. The date when it was first introduced.
d. The name of the president who was in office then.
e. The sales generated by the Air Force 1 model since 1982 and Nike's profit margin.
f. How often Nike releases a new AF1 model.
g. The number of pairs of shoes produced for each new model and the number of pairs each US store receives.
h. Where the shoes are made.
i. The profit made by Nike for each pair of AF1 sold.

4 Make sure you have understood the article

a. What is the "Air Force 1"?
b. Is it a new model?
c. Is it still popular?
d. Is it a profitable article for Nike?
e. Why is it such a success?

PART 2: ENGLISH LANGUAGE

1 Les chiffres

a. Complétez les phrases suivantes avec des chiffres trouvés dans le texte.

– Nike introduced the first Air Force 1 in the early ....'s, in ....

– In .... years, the shoe has made $ .... in sales.

– Nike releases a new Air Force 1 every .... months and sends .... to .... pairs of shoes in the USA, ... to .... to each store.

– The company sells each pair to retailers for $............, but pays only $............ to make them in Asia.

b. Lisez ces phrases à haute voix.

2 La reformulation

Reformulez les phrases suivantes en utilisant des expressions du texte pour les mots soulignés.

a. The first Air Force 1 was introduced <u>in 1982</u>.

....

b. New Air Force 1 releases sell <u>very quickly</u>.

....

c. Nike makes consumers desire the shoes by releasing only a limited number of shoes, with little promotion.

....

d. The Air Force 1 is a way for Nike to make a lot of money.

....

e. The sneakers are the shoes to wear when you're a teenager living in US cities.

....

❸ Les décennies

a. Écrivez en lettres *the 1980s* : ....

b. À quelles années correspond l'expression : *early 1980s ?* ....

c. À quelles années correspond l'expression : *mid 1980s ?* ....

d. À quelles années correspond l'expression : *late 1980s ?* ....

e. Utilisez *early, mid* ou *late* pour donner votre date de naissance. ....

....

❹ La traduction de « depuis » et de « il y a »

a. Observez la phrase suivante :
Nike introduced the first Air Force 1 sneaker 25 years ago.
Quelle est la forme verbale utilisée ? Pourquoi ?

....

b. Observez la phrase suivante :
Nike has sold Air Force 1 shoes since 1982.
Quelle est la forme verbale utilisée ? Pourquoi ?

....

c. À quoi sert le complément introduit par *since ?*

....

d. Quelle préposition utilise-t-on quand on veut parler non pas du point de départ, mais du temps écoulé depuis ce point de départ jusqu'au moment présent ?

....

e. Transformez la phrase proposée (4b) en utilisant cette préposition.

....

f. Complétez les phrases suivantes en employant *for, since* ou *ago.*

- Ronald Reagan was in office many years ....
- I have worn AF1 shoes .... 2004.
- The shoes were very popular 20 years ....
- The AF1 design has been unchanged .... several years.
- No athlete has promoted this Nike sneaker .... the days of Michael Jordan.

5 L'emploi des prépositions

a. Complétez le texte qui suit avec les prépositions suivantes : *in front of – to – in – at – of – by – since – for – over*. Certaines prépositions peuvent être utilisées plusieurs fois.

The Air Force 1 shoe was launched .... Nike .... 1982. It was the first Nike shoe .... use the Nike Air technology. The name is a reference .... Air Force 1, the plane that carries the President .... the United States of America all .... the world.

The shoes are one .... the most popular items .... cities and many suburban areas. The AF1 has been hot .... 25 years, ... 1982. New shoes are released .... weekends, and teenagers queue .... hours .... the stores .... be sure they will get a pair .... their favorite sneakers.

.... some years, Nike has offered its customers the opportunity .... design their own Air Force 1 shoe.

b. Traduisez le texte ci-dessus.

6 L'ordre des mots dans les phrases interrogatives

Observez la phrase suivante :
Does Nike make profits with the AF1 sneaker?
La réponse à la question est : *Yes, it does.*

a. Transformez les phrases suivantes en questions auxquelles on répondra par « oui » ou par « non ».

– The company releases new models every year.

....

– They have made $1 billion profits since 1982.

....

– Ronald Reagan was elected president in 1980.

....

– In the past Nike paid athletes to promote its products.

....

– Next month the new AF1 will sell in hours.

....

b. Que remarquez-vous concernant l'ordre des mots dans une phrase interrogative ?

....

7 Civilisation

▶ Survival kit, p. 189

Answer the following questions in English about politics in the USA.

a. Who is the current president of the USA? And who is the vice-president? Are they Democrats or Republicans?

....

b. What are the president's powers?

....

c. Choose from the following list presidents who were in office after Ronald Reagan (1981-1989): J.F. Kennedy, Gerald Ford, Theodore Roosevelt, Robert Nixon, Bill Clinton, Abraham Lincoln, Jimmy Carter.

....

d. Who was the first president of the USA?

....

e. What is 'the White House'? Where is it situated?

....

f. How is power shared in the USA?
- Who has executive power?

....

- Who has legislative power?

....

- Who has judiciary power?

....

PART 3: PRACTISING FOR THE EXAM

❶ Faites un compte rendu oral du texte

Survival kit, p. 171

a. Préparez l'introduction.
b. Faites un plan du texte.
1. Facts concerning Nike's AF1
2. Reasons for enduring success

c. Préparez la conclusion.

❷ Présentez en français

Survival kit, p. 173

Votre objectif est de présenter en français les raisons qui expliquent la longévité du succès de l'AF1.

❸ Rédigez un résumé du texte en français en 130 mots

Survival kit, p. 173

❹ Branching out

Survival kit, p. 181

a. Faites une recherche sur l'entreprise Nike, sur le site de Wikipedia, l'encyclopédie collaborative (http://en.wikipedia.org).
b. Constituez une fiche sur Nike, en recherchant les points suivants :
- l'identité de Nike ;
- les dates importantes dans l'histoire de l'entreprise (1964, 1971, 1982, 1984, 1988, 1990, 1998, 2003, 2004) ;
- l'histoire et la symbolique du logo.

Document 7

Vodafone Learns Hard Lessons in Japan

Outdated headsets and poor service drive away Japanese users.

Tokyo – Service problems, a poor introduction of its third-generation phone network and a limited variety of new handsets have driven away many Japanese customers of Vodafone, the world's largest cellphone carrier.

Vodafone's problems in Japan are a lesson in how global corporations can get into trouble if they try to push a single sales agenda across many national markets.

By offering the same phones to many of its 165 million worldwide subscribers, Vodafone hoped to reduce handset prices.

But the one-size-fits-all approach failed here. Japan has the most advanced terminals in the world. Consumers are used to getting new technologies like high-resolution color screens, two-megapixel cameras and full Internet access a year or two before the rest of the world.

Vodafone, which is based in London, now must win back customers if it is to revive what was once one of its most profitable units, which has fallen far behind its two larger rivals in Japan, NTT DoCoMo and KDDI.

"Japan has been a peculiar place where things haven't worked Vodafone's way," said a telecom analyst. "The company was slow to realize that Japan is really different from Europe."

Now, to revive its fortunes, Vodafone has changed the management in Tokyo, started a series of product redesigns and poured more money into its cellular networks. But the situation will only get tougher in Japan's increasingly saturated market.

Vodafone's spokesman in Japan, Matthew Nicholson, said the company was trying to make its phones more appealing. "Tailoring phones to customers in Japan is a priority," Mr Nicholson says. "We learned a lot from what happened."

Adapted from *The New York Times*, 24 September 2005.

outdated: vieillot
headset: casque
handset: combiné
to drive away: éloigner
single: unique
sales agenda: programme commercial
one-size-fits-all: modèle unique
to fail: échouer
tough: difficile
appealing: attractif
to tailor: faire du sur mesure

Faites un compte rendu oral en anglais de ce texte.

Survival kit, p. 171

Document 8

Seb se tourne vers le marché chinois

Le groupe français d'électroménager, qui ferme des usines en France, mise désormais sur la Chine, où il espère une accélération de son développement.

Après avoir résisté tant bien que mal aux assauts de la concurrence asiatique, Seb cède finalement à la tentation chinoise. Le groupe français d'électroménager a confirmé, hier, la prise de contrôle du numéro un chinois d'articles de cuisine, Zhejiang Supor Cookware. L'objectif : profiter d'un marché local en forte croissance et de faibles coûts de production.

Seb va ainsi payer 240 millions d'euros, financés par la dette, pour détenir, à terme, « entre 51 % et 59 % de Supor ». Avec cette acquisition, le groupe français, déjà propriétaire de Tefal, Krups, Rowenta, Moulinex et Calor, espère une « accélération » de son développement sur le marché chinois et, au-delà, une « forte croissance dans les marchés émergents, notamment en Asie du Sud-Est », où les taux d'équipement sont encore faibles.

Zhejiang Supor Cookware est en cela un partenaire idéal, puisque l'entreprise, créée en 1988, réalise les deux tiers de ses ventes en Chine et a dégagé, en 2005, un bénéfice net de 6,78 millions d'euros sur un chiffre d'affaires de 147 millions d'euros, en hausse de 46 %.

Forte concurrence asiatique

Thierry de la Tour d'Artaise, le PDG de Seb, avoue, de son côté, « ne plus espérer avoir une croissance importante » sur les marchés occidentaux, arrivés à saturation. Lui, qui a toujours défendu la valeur ajoutée et le savoir-faire des usines tricolores, n'a pas pu faire face à la déferlante asiatique dans le petit électroménager : 80 % des grille-pain vendus en France coûtent désormais moins de 30 €. Résultat, les ventes de l'inventeur de la cocotte-minute ont reculé en 2005 de 5,6 % en France et de 2,6 % dans les autres pays de l'Union européenne.

En se tournant vers la Chine, Seb ne cherche donc pas seulement des marchés porteurs. Il mise aussi sur une baisse de ses coûts de production.

Le groupe, qui emploie plus de 7 000 personnes en France, a récemment annoncé la suppression de 890 emplois, affirmant qu'il n'était plus possible d'y fabriquer les produits les plus banalisés, comme les bouilloires ou les cafetières. [...]

L'annonce du rachat de la société chinoise a été saluée à la Bourse de Paris, où le titre Seb gagnait hier 3,11 %, à 92,70 €. En revanche, cette stratégie ne plaît guère aux syndicats qui ont notamment évoqué « l'écœurement » des salariés de Seb, qui « se font virer alors que le groupe rachète des usines ».

Ouest-France, 16 août 2006.

Faites un compte rendu en anglais de cet article en suivant le plan suivant :

Introduction

1. Facts: who does what? Why?

2. Consequences for French workers

3. Reactions to Seb's decision

Conclusion

Chapter 2. Work

2

Document 1

Perks at work

Although budget restrictions have forced many companies in the USA to cut back health care and other job benefits, some firms find they have to offer ever more inventive perks and better services to attract and retain the best employees.

They focus more and more on keeping workers healthier, promoting yoga and pedometers for example to encourage workers to walk more. And they give insurance discounts for employees who take smoking-cessation classes.

More than 1 in 5 of the largest companies said, in a recent survey, they make dry cleaning or laundry services available at work, and nearly a quarter provide banking help. Some, like Google, serve free meals, and others arrange for entertainment discounts, shoe repair, cellphone bargains and on-site film developing.

Child care is, of course, critical for working moms and dads, but companies are paying increasing attention to other family members. About 1 out of 3 large companies offer elder-care assistance and 73 % of large companies reimburse employees for children's education.

According to the survey, government employers offer the highest overall level of benefits, retailers and wholesalers offer the lowest.

The Weekly Journal,
30 July 2006.

Looking for words

a. avantages (2 mots) : ....

b. réduire : ....

c. protection : ....

d. santé : ....

e. se concentrer sur : ....

f. nettoyage à sec : ....

g. blanchisserie : ....

h. accessible : ....

i. fournir : ....

j. spectacle : ....

k. cordonnerie : ....

l. téléphone portable : ....

m. bon prix : ....

n. pellicule photo : ....

o. sur place : ....

p. garde d'enfants : ....

q. soins aux personnes âgées : ....

r. étude : ....

s. détaillant : ....

t. grossiste : ....

Document 1 **Practice**

PREMIÈRE PARTIE : REPÉRAGE DE COMPRÉHENSION

1 Exprimez l'idée générale de ce document en français

2 Analysez le titre et le premier paragraphe

a. Repérez les mots clés du titre.

b. Qu'apporte le premier paragraphe par rapport au titre ? À quelles questions en *Wh-* répond-on ?

3 Repérez dans le texte

a. Le pays concerné par le phénomène.

b. La proportion d'entreprises qui offrent à leurs employés des services de teinturerie et de blanchisserie sur les lieux de travail, et des services financiers.

c. L'entreprise qui nourrit gratuitement ses employés.

d. La proportion d'entreprises qui proposent des services aux parents de leurs employés.

e. Le pourcentage d'entreprises qui remboursent les frais de scolarité des enfants.

f. Le type d'entreprises qui sont les plus généreuses et celles qui le sont le moins.

4 Vérifiez que vous avez compris

a. Citez des avantages en nature proposés par de grandes entreprises américaines.

b. Pourquoi les entreprises sont-elles aussi généreuses alors qu'elles souffrent de réductions budgétaires ?

DEUXIÈME PARTIE : REPÉRAGE DE LANGUE

1 La dérivation

Complétez les phrases suivantes à l'aide d'un mot formé à partir du verbe donné entre parenthèses.

Exemple : Employees appreciate perks (to employ).

a. .... give perks to retain the best employees (to employ).

b. Budget .... mean companies reduce their costs (to restrict).

c. .... are happy when companies care about them (to work).

d. Firms provide .... discounts to their staff (to insure).

e. .... employees are happier than others as regards perks (to govern).

f. Children's .... is expensive for parents (to educate).

2 Les comparatifs et les superlatifs

Complétez le tableau suivant en repérant dans le texte des adjectifs et des adverbes au comparatif et au superlatif.

	Comparatif	Superlatif
inventive (l. 6)		
good (l. 7)		
healthy (l. 10)		
much (l. 13)		
old (l. 35)		
high (l. 41)		
low (l. 43)		

a. Expliquez la différence de construction entre les comparatifs des adjectifs et des adverbes courts et longs.

....

b. Faites le même travail pour les superlatifs.

....

c. Complétez le tableau de la page précédente avec les formes qui manquent.

d. *Good* et *much/many* sont irréguliers. Donnez les comparatifs et les superlatifs des adjectifs irréguliers suivants.

	Comparatif	**Superlatif**
bad		
little		
far		

❸ Traduction en anglais

a. Les grandes entreprises américaines proposent à leurs personnels des avantages en nature et des services plus adaptés pour attirer et pour garder les meilleurs employés.

....

....

....

b. Selon l'article, les employés sont plus heureux dans les services publics.

....

....

c. Ils sont en meilleure santé mais leurs salaires sont inférieurs.

....

d. Aux États-Unis, les entreprises les plus populaires sont celles qui proposent à leurs salariés le niveau le plus élevé d'avantages sociaux.

....

....

TROISIÈME PARTIE : ACQUISITION DE MÉTHODES

❶ Entraînez-vous au compte rendu en anglais

▶ **Survival kit,** p. 171

a. Préparez l'introduction (origine du document et questions en *Wh-* en une phrase).

b. Faites un plan du texte.
1. Facts (Who? Does what? Where?)
2. Reasons (Why?)

c. Préparez la conclusion.

❷ Branching out

a. Your 2-year-course includes vocational training in companies to gain work experience. Does the company you are working for offer benefits and perks?

b. If you could choose the company where you'll work later, what would you favour? A better salary? More free time? Or perks?

Document 2

The Question: Should employers hire fat people?

It is estimated that, in England and Wales, 18 million working days a year are lost to obesity. Some studies also show that employees with a high body mass index (BMI) are less productive and more prone to absenteeism. Productivity and presenteeism aren't everything, of course, but Britain's employers certainly don't like fat: a new poll of 2,000 personnel officers reveals that half of them believe overweight people lack self-discipline, and that obesity affects productivity. A third think that obesity is a valid medical reason for not hiring someone.

In America, where they're ahead of us on every level of this debate, Wal-Mart is trying, it was reported yesterday, to incorporate physical exercise into every employee's job description, not to help the overweight get in shape, but to stop them applying for jobs in the first place – in their own words "to dissuade unhealthy people from coming to work at Wal-Mart".

In the UK, refusing to hire a specific fat person would be discriminatory.

The Guardian, October 28, 2005.
BTS Comptabilité et gestion des entreprises, session 2006.

---

body mass: masse corporelle
prone to: sujet à
poll: sondage
overweight: en surpoids
to hire: embaucher
to get in shape: maigrir
to apply for: postuler
unhealthy: en mauvaise santé

Document 3

Rise in office rudeness

As workloads mount and email and phone communication is increasingly used instead of face-to-face conversation, office rudeness is on the rise in the US.

From bosses who don't acknowledge employees for entire days – failing to say good morning or to leave time to talk during the day – to managers so exhausted they perpetually shout at employees, the result of office rudeness is it hurts productivity and it pushes people to leave.

According to an organizational psychologist in Alabama, rudeness is becoming more of a problem as people have to respond quicker now and they often have a lot of work to do, which causes more stress.

Rudeness at work is often a natural extension of the rudeness experienced more and more in everyday life. Incivility in the office is part of a general attitude of people thinking mainly about themselves.

Rudeness in the workplace can cost organizations time, effort and talent. More than 90% of the 3,000 employees surveyed in a study by the University of Southern California said they had experienced incivility at work. Of these, 50% said they contemplated changing jobs after several incidents. 25% cut back their efforts on the job and one in eight said they had left a company because of a rude incident.

While rudeness can hurt productivity, most cases go unreported and unnoticed by management, because there are no laws to protect employees. And yet human-resource experts say the solution is often to let people know that something is wrong.

Adapted from *The Wall Street Journal*, January 17, 2006.

---

rudeness: impolitesse
workload: charge de travail
to acknowledge: faire signe à
exhausted: épuisé
to contemplate: envisager de

Présentez ces deux textes à l'oral.

Survival kit, p. 171

Document 4

Seniors in the work force

Sean O'Connor is a Gateshead business lawyer who works part-time. After suffering from heart problems at 55, he stopped working round the clock and began reducing stress in his life. Yet, he doesn't plan to retire just yet. "There's plenty of time for that," says O'Connor, who will be 92 next month, but looks about 70.

Few of us will be working at 90, but in many ways, O'Connor, who is working with his daughter, is an example of what will happen in future. A majority of the baby-boomers say they expect to work after retirement age.

That means it will be common for seniors to keep working for the interest of the job, and to secure good incomes.

And we will need the seniors' expertise. Indeed, as millions of boomers begin retiring in the next ten years, creating job shortages in many companies, those who stay on the job will be welcome, all the more so as a lot of them will choose to work part-time, on missions, or for themselves.

And senior workers are likely to be appreciated as they are generally praised for their reliability, their punctuality, their loyalty and their experience.

Faced with fragile pension systems, rising health care costs, and shrinking birth rates, more and more organizations would like governments to increase numbers of seniors in the work force.

This can mean making it more difficult for older workers to leave the job market, by pushing back the retirement age, for example, and encouraging those who wish to stay on.

The Newcastle Journal,
20 September 2006.

Looking for words

a. main-d'œuvre : ....

b. juriste : ....

c. cœur : ....

d. 24 heures sur 24 : ....

e. retraite : ....

f. revenu : ....

g. pénurie : ....

h. bienvenu : ....

i. à temps partiel : ....

j. probable : ....

k. loué : ....

l. fiabilité : ....

m. fidélité : ....

n. santé : ....

o. en diminution : ....

p. taux de natalité : ....

q. le marché du travail : ....

r. reculer : ....

Document 4 **Practice**

PART 1: UNDERSTANDING THE TEXT

1 Give the general idea of the article

2 Analyse the title and the first paragraph

a. Give the key-words in the title.
b. What type of information can be found in the 1st paragraph?

3 Find the following information in the article

a. Sean O'Connor's age.
b. His profession.
c. Where he works.
d. How old he was when he had heart problems.
e. When he plans to retire.
f. Who he is working with.

4 Make sure you have understood the article

a. What is surprising about Sean O'Connor?
b. Does he work alone?
c. Does he work full-time?
d. According to the article, what does a majority of baby-boomers plan to do after retirement age?
e. What are their motivations?
f. Why will the seniors be welcome in companies?
g. Why are senior members of staff appreciated in companies?
h. Why are the seniors a 'cheap' and convenient workforce for companies?
i. Why will that extra workforce be financially needed in our society in future?
j. What policies are governments likely to implement to keep the seniors in activity?

PART 2: ENGLISH LANGUAGE

1 La dérivation

Complétez chaque phrase à l'aide d'un mot, trouvé dans l'article, formé à partir de l'élément donné entre parenthèses.

a. Sean O'Connor is a business .... who works in Gateshead (law).

b. A majority of the baby- .... plan to work when they are older (boom).

c. Companies will need the seniors' .... (expert).

d. Seniors are appreciated for their ...., their ...., their .... (punctual, reliable, loyal).

e. .... will encourage .... to push back legal .... age (organize, govern, retire).

2 La proposition infinitive avec *want* et *would like*

a. Comparez le français et l'anglais dans les phrases suivantes et dites si le mot « que » est traduit en anglais.

1. Les entreprises <u>voudraient que</u> les gouvernements <u>repoussent</u> l'âge de la retraite.
   Companies <u>would like</u> governments <u>to push back</u> retirement age.
2. Les seniors <u>veulent que</u> les gouvernements <u>financent</u> leurs frais de santé.
   Seniors <u>want</u> governments <u>to finance</u> their health care costs.

b. Traduisez les phrases suivantes :

– La fille de Sean O'Connor aimerait que son père prenne sa retraite car il a des problèmes cardiaques.

....

....

....

....

– L'entreprise veut que le senior utilise son expertise pour former les jeunes employés.

....

....

....

❸ Les verbes construits avec *-ing*

Observez les constructions suivantes :
– l. 5-7 : *he stopped working round the clock and began reducing stress in his life* ;
– l. 21-23 : *it will be common for seniors to keep working for the interest of the job.*
Les verbes soulignés expriment le début, la continuation ou la fin d'une action.
D'autres verbes ont la même contruction : *to like, to love, to hate, to enjoy...*

Complétez les phrases suivantes en utilisant la construction en *-ing*.

a. He will stop .... when he is 65 (to work).

b. They love .... football matches on TV (to watch).

c. He keeps .... me when we shall meet (to ask).

d. Do you enjoy .... in this course? (to study).

e. I hate .... early in the morning (to get up).

❹ Les quantités

– Comment exprimer « beaucoup »
***much* + un singulier ; *many* + un pluriel ; *a lot of, plenty of* + un singulier ou un pluriel ; *lots of* + un pluriel**
– Comment exprimer « peu »
***little* + un singulier ; *few* + un pluriel**
– Traduction de « un peu », « quelques »
***a little* + un singulier ; *a few* + un pluriel**

a. Retrouvez dans l'article des phrases avec des mots exprimant des quantités.

– L. 9 : "There's .... of time for that."

– L. 13 : .... of us will be working at 90.

– L. 29 : creating job shortages in .... companies.

– L. 32 : all the more so as .... of them will choose to work part-time.

b. Expliquez l'emploi des expressions que vous avez relevées, et traduisez-les.

....

....

....

....

c. Complétez les phrases suivantes en choisissant parmi les expressions suivantes :
a little - little - a lot of - lots of - a few - few - plenty of - many - much.

– .... companies would like governments to push back retirement age.

– I have .... work to do for tomorrow.

– The meeting was not a success, only very .... people came.

– I am glad, I have just arrived, and I have already made .... friends.

– Do .... seniors in your company plan to stay on after retirement age?

– That plant is very dry, it needs .... water.

– Be quick, I have very .... time for you!

5 L'ordre des mots dans les phrases interrogatives et les pronoms en *Wh-*

L'ordre des mots dans une phrase interrogative est : auxiliaire + sujet + verbe, sauf quand le pronom interrogatif en *Wh-* est sujet de la phrase.

Organisez les phrases suivantes en questions.

a. ? / did / Sean / have / problems / O'Connor / When / heart

....

....

b. ? / now / is / How / old / he

....

....

c. ? / will / When / millions / baby-boomers / begin / retiring / of

....

....

d. ? / fragile / pension / systems / Why / are

....

....

e. ? / costs / Which / rising / are

....

....

f. ? / will / to / choose / Who / retire

....

....

6 Les noms composés

a. Observez l'expression suivante :
Sean O'Connor is "a 92-year-old-Gateshead business lawyer".
Indiquez quel est l'ordre des mots pour qualifier le juriste.

....

b. Traduisez la phrase.

....

c. Que remarquez-vous concernant l'ordre des mots en français et en anglais ?

....

....

d. Traduisez les expressions suivantes en formant des mots composés.
- Les taux de natalité qui baissent en France.

....

....

- Les fragiles systèmes de retraite européens.

....

....

- Les coûts de protection de la santé en augmentation.

....

....

- Un étudiant de BTS 1re année âgé de 20 ans.

....

....

PART 3: PRACTISING FOR THE EXAM

❶ Faites un compte rendu oral du texte

▶ **Survival kit,** p. 171

a. Préparez l'introduction (sources, idée générale du document) en répondant aux questions en *Wh-* en une phrase.

b. Faites un plan du texte.
1. Facts (Who? Does What? Where?)
2. Reasons for the trend (Why?)
3. Prospects

c. Préparez la conclusion.

❷ Rédigez un compte rendu du texte en français en 150 mots (+/– 10 %)

▶ **Survival kit,** p. 173

❸ Branching out

▶ **Survival kit,** pp. 176-177

a. Préparez votre CV et une lettre de motivation en vue d'un stage chez Sean O'Connor.

b. Preparing for a professional interview.
You have been short-listed for work experience in Mr O'Connor's office. He says he will call you for more information. Be ready for the interview (presenting your CV, your experience, how you are suitable for the work placement).

Information concerning Sean O'Connor's business
- He is specialized in giving advice to companies, in supplier-customer relations, in setting up companies in the UK and abroad, in the evolution of company legal statutes, and in the protection of patents and copyrights.
- Address: 256 Millennium Bridge Road, Gateshead, GA5 3AD
- Phone: 00 44 191 272 76 89
- E-mail: soconnor@oal.com

Document 5

Women will <u>earn</u> the same as men – if they wait 150 years

Women could earn less than men for the next 150 years because of discrimination and ineffective government policies, according to leading economic analysts.

Thirty years after laws began to reduce the disparity between male and female pay, (...) the salaries of today's young women arc still substantially less than those of their male colleagues, and the inequality has changed little in ten years.

In the report by the Centre for Economic Performance (CEP) at the London School of Economics, the imbalance has been blamed partly on the penalisation of women who take maternity leave and work part-time after having children.

The report on women's salaries found that even those who worked full-time and did not take career breaks would earn 12% less than their male counterparts after ten years.

Alan Manning, the author of the report, said: "the problem (...) is that women are continuing to choose family over career at some point in their life".

When they return to the labour market they often work part-time. Our labour market severely punishes those who sacrifice career over family."

The report criticises the Women and Work Commission for being "not very specific" about how high-level jobs could be opened up to flexible working practices. (...) He describes some of the commission's suggestions as sensible, but adds: "I am a little sceptical about how effective their recommendations are likely to be."

The Times,
28 July 2006.

---

to earn: gagner
leading: renommé
law: loi
imbalance: déséquilibre
maternity leave: congé de maternité
part-time: à temps partiel
full-time: à temps plein
break: pause
counterpart: homologue
high-level: de haut niveau
practices: habitudes, pratiques
sensible: cohérent

Faites un compte rendu oral en anglais de ce texte.

Survival kit, p. 171

2

Document 6

Overwork is making us ill. **Sally Kinnes** on why staff are being urged to do less

Go home – please

Among the new words hauled in from current usage and pinned down in the new Collins Concise Dictionary was "presenteeism". Maybe an eager drone had stayed late in the office to ensure it was there, for presenteeism is defined as working longer hours and taking fewer holidays than the boss demands.

Who would do such a thing? Those who feel that their job is insecure, answers the man credited with coining the term – Cary Cooper, professor of organisational psychology and health at Manchester University. "When even the cutting edge industries like telecoms and IT are downsizing, you want to show commitment by getting in earlier, staying later and sending e-mails at night. Fewer people means more work, which means more stress; and that has a knock-on effect on your private life. It's a downward spiral."

Meanwhile, the escalating benefits war between firms battling to retain scarce talent is turning once drab offices into 21st century "corporate" villages boasting everything from office bars and gyms to masseurs, manicurists, play areas and even now granny crèches. The result is that, for some staff, the office can genuinely seem more appealing than home.

This combination of job insecurity and ever more enticing offices is prompting firms which once fretted over absenteeism to start worrying instead about presenteeism and staff who simply won't go home.

This may partly stem from genuine concern for the well-being of the workers, but it is also because a growing weight of evidence shows that staff who work overlong hours end up producing less rather than more. Just as workers need lunch-breaks, so, it seems, they also need a life outside the office.

British Telecom have gone further by launching an explicit campaign against presenteeism. It not only reminds staff that overtime is frowned on, but uses a management consultancy to inspect employees' timesheets and thus spot people who are spending too long at work. Other firms don't just allow but encourage staff to take "duvet days" (unscheduled days off) and paid sabbaticals. [...]

Britain works the longest hours in Europe and probably the second longest, after America, in the developed world. It's making us ill. [...]

The jargon for solving the problem of presenteeism is striking "the work-life balance" (not yet in the dictionary).

Lloyds TSB are doing their bit to promote this balance by allowing staff the option of working a significant part of the time at home.

Sally Kinnes,
The Guardian, August 16, 2001.

---

to haul in: amener
to pin down: (ici) définir
eager drone: (littéralement) bourdon empressé
cutting edge: de pointe
scarce: rare
drab: terne
to fret: s'inquiéter
to frown on: désapprouver

Looking for words

a. surmenage : ....
b. exiger : ....
c. inventer : ....
d. réduire les effectifs : ....
e. engagement : ....
f. répercussion : ....
g. avantages : ....
h. se vanter de : ....
i. attrayant : ....
j. provenir de : ....
k. heures supplémentaires : ....
l. cabinet de conseils : ....
m. semainier : ....
n. couette : ....
o. imprévu : ....
p. trouver : ....
q. équilibre : ....
r. faire sa part : ....

Document 6 **Practice**

PREMIÈRE PARTIE : REPÉRAGE DE COMPRÉHENSION

1 Exprimez l'idée générale de ce document en français

2 Analysez le titre, le sous-titre et le premier paragraphe (l. 1 à 11) Survival kit, p. 167

a. Traduisez le titre.
b. Relevez les mots-clés du sous-titre et du premier paragraphe.
c. Le titre est-il explicite ? Général ou amusant ? Dites pourquoi.

3 Repérez dans le texte

a. Le nom du dictionnaire cité dans l'article.
b. Le nom du professeur qui a inventé le mot « *presenteeism* ».
c. Le nom de l'université où il enseigne.
d. Le contraire du « présentéisme ».
e. Le nom des entreprises qui cherchent des solutions au problème du surmenage de leurs employés.
f. Les deux pays dans le monde industrialisé dans lesquels les gens travaillent le plus.

4 Vérifiez que vous avez compris

a. Quelle est la définition du « présentéisme » ?
b. Qui pratique le « présentéisme » ?
c. Pourquoi les employés passent-ils volontiers plus d'heures dans leur entreprise que jadis ?
d. Quelles sont les conséquences du surmenage ?
e. Comment les entreprises réagissent-elles ?
f. Pourquoi les entreprises réagissent-elles ?
g. Quelle est la solution pour résoudre le problème du « présentéisme » ?

DEUXIÈME PARTIE : REPÉRAGE DE LANGUE

1 Définitions

Associez chaque verbe de la liste ci-dessous (1 à 5) avec sa définition (a à e).

1. to overwork
2. to work overtime
3. to overstaff
4. to oversee
5. to have an overdraft

a. to provide with too large a staff
b. to work too much
c. to have a deficit in the bank
d. to work in addition to the regular hours
e. to supervise workers

2 L'emploi des prépositions

En vous reportant au texte si nécessaire, complétez les phrases avec les prépositions suivantes (attention, certaines peuvent être employées plusieurs fois) : *at – from – between – by – of – for – in.*

Nowadays, a lot .... people work too much because they are afraid .... losing their jobs and because they feel happy .... their offices. But some companies are concerned .... the well-being .... their employees and they look .... solutions. They promote a balance .... private and professional life, ... allowing people to stay away .... the office and to work .... home.

❸ La formation des mots en *-ion*

Complétez le texte ci-dessous avec des mots en *-ion* formés à partir des mots entre parenthèses.

People spend too many hours in their offices due to a (combine) .... of factors: the (international) .... of business makes jobs insecure, the (organise) .... of working hours is stressful, therefore people take few lunch-breaks and rarely have (converse) .... with their colleagues. Owing to the (global) .... of (communicate) ...., (inform) .... circulates quickly, with (decide) .... to be made very fast, without any (hesitate) ....

❹ Les comparatifs de supériorité et les superlatifs

Les adjectifs sont dits « courts » quand ils ont une ou deux syllabes et les adjectifs sont dits « longs » quand ils ont plus de deux syllabes.

a. Relevez dans le texte des adjectifs au comparatif de supériorité.

– Adjectifs dits « courts » :..

– Adjectifs dits « longs » :...

b. Relevez dans le texte un adjectif au superlatif.

– Adjectif court : ....

c. Comment forme-t-on le comparatif de supériorité et le superlatif d'un adjectif court ?

....

d. Comment forme-t-on le comparatif de supériorité et le superlatif d'un adjectif long ?

....

e. Certains adjectifs ont des comparatifs et des superlatifs irréguliers. Inscrivez-les dans le tableau ci-dessous.

Adjectifs	Comparatifs de supériorité	Superlatifs
much		
little		
good		
bad		
far		

f. Faites des phrases avec les mots suggérés en mettant les adjectifs soulignés au comparatif.

– people / people / French / British / <u>long</u> / work / than / hours / .

....

– people / people / French / British / <u>few</u> / holidays /than / take / .

....

– These / arrive / <u>early</u> / people / at work / than / demands / their boss / .

....

– corporate villages / Modern / are / <u>attractive</u> /offices / old / than / .

....

g. Faites des phrases avec les mots suggérés en mettant les adjectifs soulignés au superlatif.
- The / the work / long / in the world / Americans / hours / .

....

- the / solution / popular / to reduce / "Duvet days" / are / overwork / .

....

5 Les noms singuliers suivis d'un verbe au pluriel

a. Observez les expressions suivantes :
- sous-titre : *staff are being urged to do less* ;
- l. 51-52 : *staff who work overlong hours...* ;
- l. 57-58 et l. 64-65 : *British Telecom have gone further/[companies] spot people who are spending too long at work.*

b. Pour chaque phrase ci-dessus :
- entourez le sujet ;
- soulignez le verbe.

c. Que remarquez-vous ?

....

....

6 L'utilisation de *to allow*

a. Observez la phrase : *Other firms allow staff to take duvet days,* et dites quelle est la construction qui suit *allow.*

....

....

b. Remplacez *staff* par un pronom personnel.

....

c. Utilisez la même construction pour la dernière phrase du texte.
Lloyds allow...

....

....

....

7 L'expression de la cause et de la conséquence

a. Analysez la phrase suivante : *The companies react against presenteeism because staff who work too much produce less rather than more.*

> **La proposition introduite par *because* exprime la cause ; le début de la phrase est la conséquence de cet état de fait.**

b. Réécrivez cette phrase en utilisant d'autres mots de liaison exprimant la cause.

The companies react ....

....

c. Réécrivez à nouveau la phrase en insistant sur la conséquence.

Staff who work too much produce less rather than more, ...

....

d. Retrouvez deux autres expressions de la conséquence dans le texte.
- Dans le paragraphe 3 (l. 28 à 39) : ....
- Dans le paragraphe 6 (l. 57 à 69) : ....

❽ L'utilisation des pronoms interrogatifs en *Wh-*

Posez des questions sur les mots soulignés suivants.

Exemple : <u>*Britain*</u> *works the longest hours in Europe.* → ***Who*** *works the longest hours?*

– People <u>work</u> too much nowadays.

....

– <u>Staff</u> are being urged to do less.

....

– <u>Fewer people</u> means more work.

....

– Companies encourage people <u>to take duvet days</u>.

....

– Companies worry <u>because stressed staff are less efficient</u>.

....

❾ Traduction en anglais

a. Les patrons britanniques s'inquiètent car leur personnel passe plus d'heures au bureau qu'ils ne l'exigent.

....

....

....

b. Les gens restent plus longtemps dans leur entreprise car les bureaux modernes sont plus attrayants que jadis.

....

....

....

c. Les gens croient que le « présentéisme » leur permet de montrer leur engagement envers l'entreprise.

....

....

TROISIÈME PARTIE: ACQUISITION DE MÉTHODES

❶ Rédigez un compte rendu en anglais

▶ **Survival kit**, p. 173

a. Introduction

b. Plan

1. The problem (Who does what? Why?)
2. Consequences
3. Reactions

c. Conclusion

❷ Traduisez les paragraphes 4 et 5 (l. 40 à 56)

▶ **Survival kit**, p. 174

❸ Branching out

▶ **Survival kit**, p. 178

a. Do you think "presenteeism" is just a British-American problem?

b. Present your experience of work (in summer jobs, in work placements, on day-release work assignments).

c. Have you experienced or witnessed overwork and "presenteeism" in the companies where you carried out work experience?

Document 7

The temp for all seasons

The summer has traditionally been a time when the unfamiliar voices of temps are heard in offices throughout the land. But like strawberries in supermarkets, temps are no longer a seasonal feature.

A Government survey shows that, while numbers of full-time permanent employees are declining, those of temps are growing. "Temporary staffing is becoming strategic," says Chris Leonard, the founder of Tempz.com, one of the few successful dot-com launches of recent months. "Companies now have a core workforce of permanent staff and a flexible staffing strategy. It's an extension of the trend towards just-in-time resourcing. You just get in people when you need them." His picture of the labour market is confirmed by Clive Davies, the associate director of Robert Half International, another leading agency. "Companies are building a budget for temps into their labour costs," he says. "It's not just a seasonal phenomenon, although the demand for temps does go up during holiday periods. The main thing is that hiring temps enables companies to respond to sudden surges in demand for their goods or services without incurring any liabilities if it doesn't last."

There is also a generational change developing in the way individuals look at their working lives. Daniel Kasmin, the human resources director of Manpower, says: "Young people in general feel that taking on temporary work gives them more liberty to move around. The end of the job-for-life culture means they no longer see any advantage in not making the most of their years of freedom before they get committed to families and mortgages."

Although employers recognise these changes, agencies report that few have developed coherent policies for integrating temps with their workforce. The usual pattern is that a call for a temp comes through an office manager who only gives the agency a few hours notice.

The boom in temporary employment has led to a proliferation of temp agencies. There are some big brand names, but plenty of others are competing for what can be highly profitable business. Increasingly, the big agencies are becoming employers in their own right, providing holiday pay, sickness benefits and skill training for the temps on their books, and covering them for insurance.

Godfrey Golzen.
Adapted from *The Times*,
August 17, 2000,
© Times newspapers Ltd.
BTS Action commerciale, session 2001.

temp: intérimaire
seasonal feature: phénomène saisonnier
permanent employee: employé en CDI
temporary staffing: personnel en CDD
dot-com: entreprise sur Internet
just-in-time: en flux tendu
resourcing: embauche
labour costs: coûts salariaux
to incur: subir
liabilities: dette/passif
to last: durer
to get committed: être engagé
mortgage: prêt hypothécaire
sickness benefits: allocation maladie
skill training: formation professionnelle

Questions

1. Présentez ce texte à l'oral. Survival kit, p. 171

2. Rédigez un compte rendu du texte en français en 200 mots (+/– 10 %). Survival kit, p. 173

Document 8

Fujitsu supprime 16 400 emplois

RESTRUCTURATION. Dernière victime de la crise du secteur de l'électronique, le japonais Fujitsu a annoncé hier la suppression de 16 400 emplois en Asie et en Amérique du Nord, soit 10 % des effectifs. La France serait épargnée.

Le secteur de l'électronique n'en finit pas de compter ses victimes dans un contexte des plus difficiles. Le dernier blessé en date, le Japonais Fujitsu, a dévoilé hier les détails de son plan de restructuration annoncé dès dimanche. Celui-ci touchera 16 400 emplois en Asie (dont 5 000 au Japon) et en Amérique du Nord, mais « pour l'heure, aucun licenciement en France n'est prévu », assure-t-on à la direction hexagonale du groupe. En Europe, 900 personnes seront licenciées dans les filiales ICL (fabrication d'ordinateurs) et DMR (Conseil informatique).

« La situation est grave »

Le plan de restructuration de Fujitsu est néanmoins radical : presque 10 % des effectifs de la société seront supprimés. Les activités de l'entreprise seront globalement réorientées en délaissant certains domaines comme les télécommunications au profit des logiciels et services informatiques. « La situation est grave », constate dans un communiqué le président de Fujitsu, Naoyuki Akikusa. « Les secteurs des puces et des nouvelles technologies de la communication ont connu une restructuration sans précédent. »

En effet, les géants de l'électronique japonaise sont particulièrement touchés par deux feux croisés : l'économie japonaise est au plus mal (le Nikkei est à son taux le plus bas depuis dix-sept ans) et les ventes mondiales de PC ont baissé de 1,9 % par rapport à l'année dernière. Même le numéro un mondial, l'américain Dell, qui semblait il y a peu s'en sortir indemne, vient d'annoncer une charge de 742 millions de dollars dans son budget pour cause de restructurations.

Les constructeurs japonais, qui jusqu'ici s'en sortaient grâce aux exportations massives vers les États-Unis, accusent de lourdes pertes. Depuis le ralentissement de l'économie américaine et, dans une moindre mesure, européenne, Sony et Matsushita ont annoncé des résultats catastrophiques et Toshiba revoit ses prévisions à la baisse. Même NEC, le principal rival de Fujitsu dans l'archipel, a dû supprimer 4 000 postes.

Dans ce contexte, Fujitsu doit donc compter lui aussi sur les réductions de postes pour dégager à nouveau des bénéfices, prévus malgré tout pour l'exercice 2003-2004, en misant sur « un redressement graduel des technologies de l'information à partir de 2002 ». À la Bourse de Tokyo, cette annonce a fait grimper le titre de 2,8 %... mais il reste en retrait de 25 % par rapport à l'an dernier.

Le Parisien, 21 août 2001.

Questions

1. Present:
- **a.** the Fujitsu company,
- **b.** the restructuring plan and its consequences on the payroll,
- **c.** the reasons for such a plan.

2. Fujitsu's competitors on the Information Technology market:
- **a.** Who are they?
- **b.** How do they cope?

Chapter 3. **Consumers**

Document 1

Fair trade clothing at M&S

British retailer Marks & Spencer PLC has announced it is going to sell a new fair trade clothing range.

The decision is backed by research and a poll showing that ethical and health issues are becoming important factors in British consumers' buying decisions.

Nearly a third of those surveyed said they had decided against buying an item of clothing because they had concerns over where it came from or how it had been made.

M&S has already taken action to reduce the salt in its food after the Food Standards Agency said salt levels were a public health issue. The retailer reduced salt by 15% in its sandwiches, and took 250 tonnes of salt out of its food products last year.

Harriet Lamb, the executive director of the Fair Trade Foundation, said buying the new M&S clothes would create a "brighter future" for Indian cotton farmers. Under the fair trade system, farmers get a fair price for their products, with a "fair trade premium" to invest in long-term farm developments as well as social projects in their communities.

The London News, 25 March 2006.

Looking for words

a. détaillant : ....

b. SA : ....

c. commerce équitable : ....

d. gamme : ....

e. s'appuyer sur : ....

f. sondage : ....

g. santé : ....

h. question : ....

i. consommateur : ....

j. sondé : ....

k. inquiétude : ....

l. réagir : ....

m. sel : ....

n. directeur général : ....

....

o. agriculteur : ....

p. juste : ....

q. prime : ....

r. à long terme : ....

s. communauté : ....

Figures

Survival kit, p. 183

Repérez dans le texte les chiffres suivants, écrivez-les et dites-les à haute voix.

a. Une date : ....
Que remarquez-vous ?

....

b. Un pourcentage : ....

c. Une fraction : ....

d. Une centaine : ....

e. Que peut-on dire du mot *hundred* ? ....

f. Repérez la date de l'article et dites-la à haute voix.

....

Document 1 **Practice**

PREMIÈRE PARTIE : REPÉRAGE DE COMPRÉHENSION

1 Exprimez l'idée générale de ce document en français

2 Analysez le titre et le premier paragraphe (l. 1 à 4) Survival kit, p. 167

a. Repérez un nom propre dans le titre.
b. Repérez les mots-clés du titre.
c. Qu'apporte le premier paragraphe par rapport au titre ?

3 Repérez dans le texte

a. Le nom de l'entreprise concernée, son statut juridique, sa nationalité.
b. La nationalité des clients sondés.
c. La proportion des consommateurs sondés qui sont inquiets de la qualité des produits qu'ils achètent.
d. Le poids de sel retiré par M&S l'an dernier dans ses produits alimentaires.
e. La nationalité des producteurs de coton qui vont bénéficier de la décision de M&S.

4 Vérifiez que vous avez compris

a. Que va vendre l'entreprise Marks & Spencer dans ses magasins ?
b. Pourquoi l'entreprise décide-t-elle de lancer cette nouvelle ligne ?
c. Que font les clients lorsqu'ils ne sont pas sûrs de l'origine ou de la qualité de la fabrication d'un article ?
d. Que va rapporter la nouvelle ligne de vêtements aux agriculteurs indiens ?

DEUXIÈME PARTIE : REPÉRAGE DE LANGUE

1 L'emploi des formes verbales

a. Relevez une phrase au présent simple (l. 34).

....

b. Relevez une phrase au prétérit (l. 23-24).

....

c. Relevez deux phrases au *present perfect* (l. 2-3 et l. 18-19).

....

....

d. Pour chaque phrase, justifiez l'emploi de ces formes verbales.

....

2 Le style indirect

a. Relevez une phrase au style indirect avec *would* (l. 27).

....

b. Transformez la phrase au style direct en commençant par : *Harriet Lamb said : "..."*

....

c. Complétez ces deux autres phrases de l'article au style indirect.

– L. 11-14 : A third of those surveyed said .... against buying an item.

– L. 20 : The British Food Agency said food levels .... a public health issue.

d. Transformez ces phrases au style direct.

– A third of those surveyed said, "We .... against buying an item."

– The British Food Agency said, "Food levels .... a public health issue."

e. Comment transforme-t-on les verbes pour respecter la concordance des temps ?

....

❸ Les noms composés : l'ordre des mots

a. Retrouvez lignes 20-21 le mot composé qui désigne l'agence britannique des normes alimentaires.

....

b. Observez.

> **– En français, l'ordre des mots est inversé.**
> **– En anglais, on place le plus près du nom (qui se trouve à la fin) ce qui est le plus important : le secteur, puis le reste.**
> **Notez que la phrase en français est beaucoup plus longue, alors qu'elle est plus compacte en anglais.**

c. Traduisez en français les expressions suivantes.
– The public health issue

....

– The Indian social community projects

....

d. Traduisez en anglais.
– La nouvelle gamme de vêtements vendue par la chaîne M&S

....

– Le directeur général de la fondation pour le commerce équitable

....

TROISIÈME PARTIE : ACQUISITION DE MÉTHODES

❶ Entraînez-vous au compte rendu oral en anglais

▶ **Survival kit,** p. 171

a. Préparez l'introduction (source, idée générale du document) en répondant aux questions en *Wh-* en une phrase.

b. Faites un plan du texte.
1. Facts (Who does what? When?)
2. Reasons (Why?)
3. Reactions

c. Préparez la conclusion.

❷ Branching out

Connectez-vous sur le site Internet de Marks & Spencer et constituez une fiche en anglais sur l'entreprise en respectant le plan suivant :

1. The company (number of stores, payroll)
2. Philosophy and corporate values
3. Plans for the future

Document 2

Companies see boom in babies

When Ann Jones became pregnant, she went on a shopping spree. In one afternoon on Oxford Street, she bought a stroller that turns into a car seat, a tub that changes colour when the water is too hot and dozens of infant clothes. The cost: £2,000!

"Some of this stuff is really expensive, I know, but I would do anything for the needs and the safety of my baby. I want to make sure my child will have the best of everything," said Jones, 35, a J.P.Morgan Chase analyst.

The emergence of an older generation of parents with higher incomes is driving demand for upmarket baby goods including £500 strollers, state-of-the-art educational toys, and designer diaper bags.

Just as men and women are competing in their jobs, they also compete through their children. Sales of infant and preschool toys, furniture, and clothing are growing everywhere, in the USA and in Europe.

The success of baby products is being driven partly by Web sites dedicated to parents' issues, with forums discussing the merits of popular products.

"Age 0 to 4 is where the money is," said a consultant in an US investment firm. "The market is growing, and there are profits to be made."

The West End News, 28 April 2006.

---

pregnant: enceinte
stroller: poussette
tub: baignoire
stuff: (ici) article
income: revenu
upmarket: haut de gamme
state-of-the-art: à la pointe de la technologie
diaper bag: sac à couche
furniture: mobilier
issue: sujet de discussion

Document 3

The pet economy

Dogs have become a brand's best friend and it's increasingly cool for cats to look as *à la mode* as their owners. […]

In the third quarter of 2000, French company Dog Generation, set up by former Givenchy executives Laurent Jugeau and Étienne Swart, launched a unisex perfume for cosseted canines called Oh My Dog! Those who thought it was a gimmick were immediately proved wrong, as Oh My Dog! became the top-selling scent of any kind in Parisian store Bon Marché during the month of September. Each bottle costs around €40. [...]

"We are positioning it as an affordable luxury," says Dog Generation president Laurent Jugeau.

"Our message to consumers is that it is a top of the range perfume, it is 100% safe and that it reflects a close relationship. It is a gift from owners to their dogs. It will never be sold in pet stores because it's an ambiguous product. We know that some people are buying it for themselves. They love the fragrance."

Dog Generation has invested €38,000 in a print advertising campaign, but most of the marketing focus has been on point of sale and public relations. Much of the perfume's success stemmed from the fact that it is marketed in the same way as other fashionable brands.

This is hardly surprising when one considers that fashion brands themselves have also moved into the dog accessories market. Burberry, for instance, produces a glossy brochure to promote its "Canine Collection", which aside from obvious items such as leads and collars extends to trouser suits and raincoats. […]

Robert Gray, *Strategieseurope*, n° 4, January 2001.

---

to cosset: choyer
gimmick: astuce publicitaire
fragrance: parfum
to stem from: provenir de
lead: laisse pour chien

Présentez ces deux textes à l'oral.

Survival kit, p. 171

3

Document 4

McDonald's Sells, Beefless, in India

BOMBAY – McDonald's Corp.'s familiar golden arches are seen in just <u>a handful of</u> Indian cities, but the world's largest fast-food chain is rapidly making inroads into the potentially huge market – all without selling a single beefburger.

Four years after McDonald's opened its first restaurant in India, it appears to have gained acceptance in a country deeply conscious both of price and of food taboos.

Its Indian outlets cater to some 3.2 million customers a month, <u>steering clear of</u> beef and pork products and using eggless recipes for their mayonnaise.

Cows are sacred to Hindus who make up most of India's 1 billion people, while Muslims are forbidden by their religion from eating pork. Many Indians are vegetarian, and particular that their food is cooked separately from meat.

"McDonald's has respected our local culture," said Amit Jatiya, the vegetarian managing director of Hardcastle Restaurants, the McDonald's joint venture in western India. "Meat and vegetarian processing and cooking are segregated."

The outlets serve only chicken, fish, mutton and vegetarian items. The Big Mac's beefless Indian cousin is a mutton burger called the Maharaja Mac. [...]

"We've proved that there is a place for the burger in India," said Vikram Bakshi, head of Connaught Plaza Restaurants Private Ltd., McDonald's joint venture in Delhi. "When we launched in 1996, many wondered if such a westernized product would fit in with Indian food habits."

A McDonald's spokesman in Illinois added: "We're extremely pleased with our success in India." The spokesman described India as an important market for McDonald's and "we have established a solid base from which to grow." Over half of McDonald's sales come from outside the United States. [...]

In a country where one can get a full meal in an inexpensive restaurant for less than $1, McDonald's has had to be careful with its pricing. Meals typically cost half of a U.S. McDonald's meal, the company said.

Reuters.
December 8, 2000.
BTS Comptabilité et gestion, session 2001.

---

a handful of: quelques
to steer clear of: éviter

Looking for words

a. entrer sur un marché : ....

b. vendre : ....

c. point de vente : ....

d. servir : ....

e. recette : ....

f. constituer : ....

g. directeur général : ....

h. co-entreprise : ....

i. transformer : ....

j. article : ....

k. chef/directeur : ....

l. lancer : ....

m. porte-parole : ....

n. ventes : ....

o. repas : ....

p. prix/tarifs : ....

Document 4 **Practice**

PREMIÈRE PARTIE : REPÉRAGE DE COMPRÉHENSION

1 Exprimez l'idée générale de ce document en français

2 Analysez le titre et le premier paragraphe (l. 1 à 8)

Survival kit, p. 167

a. Notez que le titre est explicite. Répondez aux questions :
- Qui ?
- Fait quoi ?
- Où ?
- Comment ?

b. Quelles informations complémentaires le premier paragraphe apporte-t-il ?

3 Repérez dans le texte

a. La date d'ouverture du premier restaurant McDonald's en Inde.
b. Le nombre de villes du pays où est implanté McDonald's.
c. Le nombre de clients mensuels.
d. Le nombre d'habitants du pays.
e. Le prix d'un repas dans un restaurant local bon marché.
f. Le prix d'un repas chez McDonald's aux États-Unis et en Inde.
g. La part de marché de McDonald's en dehors des États-Unis.

4 Vérifiez que vous avez compris

a. Quels sont les problèmes que l'entreprise rencontre en Inde concernant :
- les tabous religieux ?
- le prix ?

b. Que vend-on chez McDonald's en Inde ?
c. Qu'est-ce que le Maharaja Mac ?
d. Quel est le statut juridique de McDonald's en Inde ?

DEUXIÈME PARTIE : REPÉRAGE DE LANGUE

1 L'emploi des formes verbales

a. Observez la forme verbale soulignée dans chaque phrase : dites à quel temps elle est, puis expliquez pourquoi elle est utilisée.
- McDonald's <u>is making</u> inroads into [...] India. (L. 5-6)

....

- Four years after McDonald's <u>opened</u> its first restaurant in India. (L. 9-10)

....

- Outlets <u>cater</u> to some 3.2 million customers a month. (L. 15-16)

....

- McDonald's <u>has respected</u> our local culture. (L. 28-29)

....

- The outlets <u>serve</u> only chicken, fish, mutton... (L. 36-37)

....

- We've <u>proved</u>... (L. 41)

....

3

b. Quelle forme verbale choisissez-vous pour les phrases suivantes ? Conjuguez le verbe indiqué entre parenthèses.

- McDonald's sert des repas dans 28 000 restaurants dans 120 pays. (serve)

....

- Ray Kroch a ouvert le premier restaurant McDonald's à Des Plaines (Illinois) en 1955. (open)

....

- Ce lieu est devenu un musée à la gloire du fondateur. (become)

....

- Des milliers de gens dans le monde sont en train de manger un Big Mac ou un Maharaja Mac en ce moment ! (eat)

....

- L'entreprise McDonald's assure à ses actionnaires une rentabilité (retour sur investissement) élevée. (guarantee)

....

c. Traduisez les phrases de l'exercice précédent (1b) en anglais.

- ....
- ....
- ....
- ....
  ....
- ....
- ....

❷ La traduction de « depuis » et de « il y a »

a. Observez la phrase suivante : *Mc Donald's opened its first restaurant four years ago.* Quelle est la forme verbale utilisée ? Pourquoi ?

....

....

b. Observez la phrase suivante : *McDonald's has been in India since 1996.* Quelle est la forme verbale utilisée ? Pourquoi ?

....

....

c. À quoi sert le complément introduit par *since ?*

....

d. Quelle préposition utilise-t-on quand on veut parler non pas du point de départ, mais du temps écoulé depuis ce point de départ jusqu'au moment présent ?

....

e. Transformez la phrase proposée (2b) en utilisant cette préposition.

....

f. Complétez les phrases suivantes en employant *for, since* ou *ago.*

- Cows have been sacred in India .... a very long time.
- Ray Kroc opened the first McDonald's restaurant more than 50 years ....
- Amit Jatiya has worked for McDonald's .... 1997.

g. Complétez les phrases suivantes avec le verbe entre parenthèses.

– They .... to India 5 years ago. (come)

– They .... for McDonald's since the mid 1990s. (work)

– The company .... a solid base since it .... 4 years ago. (establish/arrive)

❸ Le style indirect

a. Relisez les commentaires au style direct de deux responsables indiens, Amit Jatiya (l. 28 à 35) et Vikram Bakshi (l. 41 à 50), et du porte-parole de l'entreprise McDonald's (l. 52 à 58).

b. Réécrivez le commentaire d'Amit Jatiya au style indirect en commençant par :

– *He says* ....

....

....

– *He said* ....

....

....

c. Que remarquez-vous concernant la concordance des temps ?

....

....

d. Réécrivez à présent au style indirect les commentaires de Vikram Bakshi et du porte-parole de McDonald's, en commençant par :

– *Vikram Bahshi said* ....

....

....

– *The spokesman added* ....

....

....

e. Que remarquez-vous concernant les pronoms personnels ?

....

❹ L'emploi des prépositions

Complétez le texte ci-dessous avec des prépositions.

Four years .... McDonald's arrived .... India, a spokesman says the company is very pleased .... its success there. It is a solid base .... which to grow. .... first, the company wondered whether a US product would fit in .... Indian traditions. It had to adapt .... local food taboos. Indeed, cows are sacred .... India, and Hindus cook their food separately .... meat. But there is a place .... the McDonald's burger .... India!

3

❺ Les noms composés : l'ordre des mots

a. Retrouvez, dans le premier paragraphe de l'article (l. 1 à 8), une expression qui désigne l'entreprise et qui la caractérise par son secteur et sa taille.

....

b. Observez.

> **– En français, l'ordre des mots est inversé (« la chaîne de restauration rapide la plus grande du monde »).**
> **– En anglais, on place le plus près du nom (qui se trouve à la fin) ce qui est le plus important : le secteur, puis le reste.**
> **Notez qu'en français, la phrase est longue et comporte des propositions relatives, alors qu'elle est beaucoup plus compacte en anglais.**

c. Construisez des mots composés avec les mots suivants :
- burger / mutton / popular / McDonald's / Maharaja

....

- global / corporate / McDonald's / strategy

....

❻ Les conjonctions *while* (tandis que) et *whereas* (alors que)

Complétez les phrases suivantes avec l'une ou l'autre conjonction (*while* ou *whereas*), sachant que *whereas* exprime une opposition.

- Americans eat beef .... Hindus don't. They are vegetarians.
- Hindus don't eat beef .... Muslims don't eat pork.
- We are presently studying .... others are working in companies.
- Is it all right if I listen to music .... you're working?

❼ Traduction en anglais

a. McDonald's a ouvert son premier restaurant en Inde il y a quatre ans.

....

b. La plupart des Indiens sont Hindous et ne mangent pas de bœuf, tandis que les Musulmans ne mangent pas de porc.

....

....

c. Beaucoup de gens ont été surpris quand la première chaîne de restauration rapide a lancé des burgers végétariens.

....

....

TROISIÈME PARTIE : ACQUISITION DE MÉTHODES

❶ Faites un résumé en français

▶ Survival kit, p. 173

Cherchez les idées contenues dans chaque paragraphe de l'article. Faites ce travail dans l'ordre chronologique du texte et rédigez ensuite le résumé (100 mots maximum).

❷ Branching out

▶ Survival kit, p. 180

a. Connectez-vous sur le site Internet (www.mcdonalds.com) pour rechercher si McDonald's est une entreprise citoyenne.

b. Faites une présentation en anglais sur ce thème.

Document 5

Singled-minded firms

By 2021, a third of UK households will be people living alone and big stores are already thinking small

A report published last week by the food giant Unilever and the Institute for Public Policy Research (IPPR), a think tank, highlighted the huge increase in single-person households. By 2021, more than a third of the population (35%) would live alone, it said.

The proportion of income spent by single-person households on alcohol, tobacco and recreational drugs (such as slimming aids) is noticeably higher than for those living with others. The same is true, rather more predictably for spending on gas and electricity and going out in the evening.

For big business, this remarkable population shift presents an interesting set of challenges, particularly because people buying for one are frequently unable to take advantage of the sorts of special offers and bulk discounts that those living with families or part of larger households are able to enjoy.

A spokesman for J. Sainsbury pointed out a number of areas in which the grocer has been trying to appeal more to those living on their own. For example, the supermarket has doubled its range of 25cl bottles of wine and increased the number of stores that stock them.

Unilever has also been steadily introducing new ways of packing its products to make life easier for those living alone. For example, it produces single servings of ready-made soup.

But it is not just in the food industry that companies have to cater for this new social breed. Those choosing to live solo are living in smaller homes, a fact that has not been lost in the leading DIY chains.

The report also pointed out that those living by themselves were less likely to own white goods, such as fridges and washing machines, than those living with others.

It argued that the change was making a big contribution to the rise in inequality in British society.

The Sunday Times, October 30, 2005.
BTS Management des unités commerciales, épreuve orale 2006.

---

household: foyer
to highlight: souligner
single-person: célibataire
income: revenu
slimming: amaigrissant
predictably: comme on peut s'y attendre
bulk: achats en grosses quantités
to appeal to: séduire
single serving: portion pour une personne
to cater for: satisfaire
breed: catégorie
DIY (Do It Yourself) chain: chaîne de bricolage
white goods: électroménager
to argue: soutenir

Faites un compte rendu oral de ce texte en anglais.

Survival kit, p. 171

Document 6

Credit card firm targets teens

MASTERCARD was accused yesterday of encouraging teenagers to go into debt with the launch of a payment card for children.

The world's biggest credit card group is issuing pre-payment cards to allow youngsters to purchase products on plastic.

How much the teenagers can spend is limited by the amount that their parents are prepared to deposit in advance but the scheme was described yesterday by consumer groups as "irresponsible".

The National Consumer Council (NCC) has raised fears that the cards will get children so used to spending money that is not theirs that they will go hopelessly into debt once they are old enough to apply for a credit card. Supporters, however, regard the cards as the natural step in an increasingly cashless society. They argue that the prepayment cards will familiarise children with plastic without spending too much (…).

NCC officials also expressed concern at the level of charges made by MasterCard. Customers are charged a £9.95 fee just for opening their card account and pay 85p for each withdrawal that they make from an ATM cash dispenser. Card holders are penalised with a £4.99 fee for cancelling an account or ordering a replacement card.

Phil Davies, the director of business development at MasterCard Europe, defended the Splash cards as a starter kit for financial prudence. He said: "Parents can control the amount of money their son or daughter spends on the card by limiting the amount of money placed on the card."

The minimum age for holding a card is 13. They are used in the same way as credit and debit cards but users should not be able to go into debt with them because only funds already paid into the card account can be spent.

Parents can apply to get cards for their children online.

The Times, January 26, 2006.
BTS Assistant de direction, session 2006.

Looking for words

a. cibler : ....
b. adolescent (2 mots) : ....
c. lancement : ....
d. émettre/sortir/lancer : ....
e. acheter : ....
f. projet : ....
g. association de consommateurs : ....
h. crainte : ....
i. complètement : ....
j. sans argent liquide : ....
k. soutenir que : ....
l. inquiétude : ....
m. niveau : ....
n. montant : ....

Looking for specific banking vocabulary

a. carte de paiement : ....
b. carte avec paiement à l'avance : ....
c. carte bancaire : ....
d. somme (d'argent) : ....
e. déposer : ....
f. s'endetter : ....
g. faire une demande de carte : ....
h. frais financier : ....
i. faire payer : ....
j. commission : ....
k. compte en banque : ....
l. retrait : ....
m. distributeur automatique (DAB) : ....
....
n. possesseur de carte : ....
o. fermer le compte : ....
p. une nouvelle carte : ....
q. fonds : ....

Document 6 **Practice**

PART 1: UNDERSTANDING THE TEXT

1 Give the general idea of the article

2 Analyse the title

Survival kit, p. 167

a. Who does what?

b. What other details can be found in the 1st paragraph?

3 Find the following information in the article

a. The name of the credit card group.

b. Its position on the market.

c. The type of card it is launching.

d. The name of the consumer association accusing Mastercard.

e. What the £9.95 fee is for.

f. What the 85p. charge is for.

g. How much users pay to cancel or to renew the card.

h. The minimum age for having a card.

4 Make sure you have understood the article

a. Who is the credit card group Mastercard targeting with its new card?

b. How is the card funded?

c. How can parents apply to get the card?

d. Why is the card considered as 'irresponsible' by consumer groups?

e. What is the risk for later?

f. How do supporters respond to the accusation?

g. How much does Mastercard charge for the card?

PART 2: ENGLISH LANGUAGE

1 Le vocabulaire concernant des opérations bancaires

Complétez le paragraphe suivant en utilisant les verbes qui vous sont proposés :
to open – to cancel – to hold – to apply – to pay – to be charged – to spend – to order – to deposit – to withdraw.

With the new Mastercard pre-payment card, parents can contact the bank to .... for a card. They .... £9.95 when they .... the card account. They .... money on the account. Teenagers .... the money paid onto the card by their parents. Each time card-holders .... cash from an ATM machine, they .... 85 pence, and £4.99 more when they .... the account or when they .... a new card. Teenagers can .... a card when they are 13.

2 Les pronoms personnels, les adjectifs et les pronoms possessifs

Complétez le paragraphe suivant avec les pronoms personnels (sujets ou compléments), les adjectifs ou les pronoms possessifs qui conviennent.

Clara is 16 years old. .... is going to ask .... parents to open a pre-payment card account for .... And ....

boyfriend Steven, who is 17, will ask .... parents to do the same for ....

With this card, Clara and Steven (= ....) will spend money that doesn't belong to .... but to .... parents. Nevertheless, the card belongs to ...., it is .... It will allow .... to make .... own purchases without having to ask Mum and Dad for cash each time .... want to go shopping.

"It's fantastic for Steven and me (= for ....)," Clara says, "the card is .... I think .... will teach .... how to live in a cashless society."

"Yes," Clara's mother adds, " .... hope it will teach .... how to manage .... budget when .... earn .... own money."

❸ Le passif

a. Relevez les phrases à la forme passive dans le texte.
- L. 1 : Mastercard ...
- L. 9 : The scheme ...
- L. 21-22 : Customers ...
- L. 24-25 : Card holders ...
- L. 34 : They ...
- L. 36 : Only funds already paid into the card ...

b. Soulignez la forme verbale.

....

c. Comment construit-on le passif en anglais ?

....

d. Expliquez l'utilisation des formes verbales.

....

....

....

e. Une seule de ces phrases est suivie d'un complément d'agent. Laquelle ? Pourquoi ?

....

....

f. Pourquoi les autres phrases à la forme passive n'ont-elles pas de complément d'agent ?

....

....

❹ Les modaux

> **– *Can* et son équivalent *to be able to* expriment la possibilité physique et intellectuelle.**
> **– *May* exprime la permission ou l'éventualité, et son équivalent *to be allowed to* exprime l'autorisation.**
> **– *Must* exprime l'obligation, *to have to* l'obligation imposée par les circonstances.**

Les auxiliaires de modalité :
– n'ont pas d'infinitif ;
– ne prennent pas de *-s* à la 3e personne du singulier du présent ;
– ont des formes interrogatives et négatives sans *do* ;
– sont suivis d'un verbe à l'infinitif sans *to* ;
– n'ont pas de participe présent, ni de participe passé.

Observez les phrases suivantes et expliquez l'emploi de l'auxiliaire de modalité.
– "Mum! Can I use your credit card?" Clara asks.

....

– "Yes, you can, you certainly can... but you may not!" the mother answers.

....

– Parents can apply for the card online, their children will be able to pay with debit cards.

....

– Teenagers have to pay fees when they withdraw cash.

....

– Parents must control their children don't go into debt.

....

5 La forme interrogative

a. Transformez les phrases suivantes en questions auxquelles on répondra par « oui » ou par « non ».
– Mastercard was accused yesterday of encouraging teenagers to go into debt.

....

– The credit card company is launching a pre-paid card for teenagers.

....

– Consumer groups regard the card as "irresponsible".

....

– The cards will familiarise children with plastic money.

....

b. Que remarquez-vous concernant l'ordre des mots dans les phrases interrogatives ?

6 Les prépositions

Complétez le paragraphe ci-dessous en choisissant parmi les prépositions qui vous sont proposées. Attention, certaines prépositions peuvent être utilisées plusieurs fois, et d'autres pas du tout. *Of - by - with - without - at - in - to - for - against - into - out - of - on - from.*

.... its new pre-payment card, the Mastercard company is accused .... a consumer group .... encouraging teens to spend too much.

.... the past, children used to get pocket money .... their parents, whereas nowadays, ... this card, they can spend the money their parents have deposited .... their account.

3

Supporters say the card will familiarise young people .... plastic money, as we live .... a society where more and more purchases are made .... card, ... using cash.

And the risk .... users .... going .... debt is limited as only funds already paid .... the card account can be spent.

❼ Traduction en anglais

a. Avec cette carte prépayée, les adolescents pourront faire des achats sans utiliser d'argent liquide.

....

....

b. Les parents doivent-ils payer pour ouvrir et fermer un compte ?

....

....

c. Les dépenses des enfants peuvent être contrôlées.

....

....

d. Peux-tu m'autoriser à ouvrir un compte ?

....

....

e. Les jeunes devront payer une commission à chaque retrait d'un distributeur automatique.

....

....

PART 3: PRACTISING FOR THE EXAM

❶ Faites un compte rendu oral du texte

▶ **Survival kit,** p. 171

a. Préparez l'introduction (sources, idée générale du document) en répondant aux questions en *Wh-* en une phrase.

b. Faites un plan du texte.
1. Facts (Who does what?)
2. Negative reactions to the cards
3. The supporters' views

c. Préparez la conclusion.

❷ Traduisez le texte en français (l. 1 à 12 jusqu'à "*credit card*").

▶ **Survival kit,** p. 174

❸ Branching out

a. Can teenagers get similar cards in France?

b. According to you, what is the goal of the company, when it launches a credit card for teenagers?

c. What are the advantages and the drawbacks of using plastic money (for customers, for shops)?

Document 7

Got 5,000 euros? Need a new car?

Drivers across Europe are clamouring for Renault's ultracheap, no-frills Logan

A strange thing happened when French automaker Renault last fall rolled out the no-frills Logan, a midsize model designed to sell for as little as 5,000 euros ($6,000) in emerging markets like Poland. Western buyers clamoured for the car.

So this June, Renault began delivering the roomy, unpretentious five-seater to France, Germany, and Spain. The pricier West European version includes a passenger-side airbag and a three-year warranty but still sells for a base price of $9,300 – about half that of the Ford Focus ($17,250) and the Volkswagen Golf ($18,264).

Building cheap cars for the West wasn't what Chairman Louis Schweitzer had in mind when he spent $592 million in 1999 to acquire and retool ailing Romanian automaker Dacia. He aimed to produce a low-cost vehicle targeted at developing countries, home to 80% of consumers who have never owned a car.

But he may well have met with a rich vein of demand in the West for utilitarian cars, part of the discount mania that has spread across Europe.

The simple design means assembly at the Romanian plant is done almost entirely without robots. That lets Renault capitalize on the country's low labor costs. Gross pay for a Dacia line worker is $324 per month, vs an average $4,723 a month for auto workers in Western Europe.

Other companies are working on cheap cars, too. Volkswagen is considering building a $3,650 car for China. India's Tata motor is expected to debut a $2,000 car before 2008. But for now, the Logan is the one turning heads.

Business Week, July 4, 2005.
BTS Management des unités commerciales, session 2006.

---

to clamour for: réclamer
no-frills: basique
roomy: spacieux
warranty: garantie
to retool: rééquiper
ailing: en difficulté
to target: cibler
to own: posséder
labor costs: coûts salariaux
gross: brut
line worker: ouvrier sur une chaîne de montage
average: moyenne

Faites un compte rendu oral de ce texte en anglais.

Survival kit, p. 171

3

Document 8

Pour tout l'or des seniors

Des voitures haut de gamme, des voyages organisés, des croisières de luxe et bien sûr des produits de beauté pour rester jeunes, les baby-boomers tirent leur révérence, mais leurs revenus, supérieurs à la moyenne des Français, suscitent les convoitises des entreprises.
Le papy-boom... un bain de jouvence pour l'économie

À eux deux, Aline et Jean, 60 et 63 ans, à la retraite, gagnent 4 200 euros par mois. Leurs deux filles, même s'ils continuent à les aider, sont sorties d'affaire. Ils ont quasiment fini de payer leur appartement de banlieue, ils peuvent presque tout dépenser. Ils ne s'en privent pas. Cet été, ils ont loué une maison en Bretagne et un gîte rural dans les Cévennes. Ils font souvent des allers-retours à Marseille, où ils ont de bons amis. Ils achètent sur eBay. [...] Quand ils ne voyagent pas, ils lisent, vont au cinéma, au théâtre. Jean compose des chansons, reprend des cours d'anglais et d'espagnol. Sa femme vient deux fois par semaine à Paris pour voir des expositions de peinture. Elle songe à devenir bénévole dans une association, mais pas tout de suite. « Pour nous deux, c'est une véritable seconde vie », explique-t-elle en souriant.

Des privilégiés, Aline et Jean ? Pas du tout. Ce couple a même le profil type des Français qui se sont retirés de la vie active. Désendettés, dotés de budgets confortables et d'une bonne santé, ils ont le plus souvent bénéficié d'un petit héritage. Voilà pourquoi ils croquent la vie à pleines dents.

Bien sûr, la France compte encore près de 622 000 retraités qui perçoivent le minimum vieillesse, 588 euros par mois pour une personne seule, 1 054 euros pour un couple [...].

Il n'empêche [...]. Selon l'Insee, en moyenne, les 55-64 ans dépensent 31 251 euros par an. Les 65-74 ans 22 453 euros. « Ils sont vraiment riches entre 50 et 65 ans. Ceux-là disposent de revenus supérieurs de 30 % par rapport à la moyenne des Français », précise Hervé Sauzay, le directeur du département Générations du groupe Bayard-Presse, qui édite le mensuel *Notre Temps* (906 000 exemplaires). Ces retraités-là disposent d'un pouvoir d'achat de plus de 152 milliards d'euros, selon Audika, le numéro un de la correction auditive en France ! [...]

Selon le CREDOC*, les sexagénaires représentent 60 % des départs en voyages organisés, le quart des trajets en avion, 70 % des achats de camping-cars, 80 % des voitures haut de gamme et 50 % du marché des produits de beauté.

D'après *Le Nouvel Observateur*, Martine Gilson, octobre 2006.

*CREDOC : Centre de Recherche pour l'Étude et l'Observation des Conditions de vie.

Questions

1. Have all French pensioners got the same living pattern? Justify your answer.

2. How do French affluent pensioners spend their money?

3. What sectors of the economy benefit from this 'fountain of youth'?

Chapter 4. Distribution

4

Document 1

"Ding-Dong." The Avon Lady is back!

Move over, Tupperware! Food, gadgets, jewellery, pet products, clothing and toys are now being sold at parties of families and friends by home-based entrepreneurs.

The Direct Selling Association estimates that in the United States alone, more than 13.6 million people are in the business, most of them part-time. Sales represented nearly $30 billion last year.

Even Body Shop, a traditional cosmetics retailer, has started direct-sales units, with products that are identical to those sold in stores. The idea is to inject the personal touch into an increasingly impersonal retailing world.

This type of direct selling has been a popular fixture in the USA since the 1950s when Tupperware and Avon ladies were regular visitors at American homes selling plastic boxes and beauty products.

The current popularity of direct sales is connected to social changes. As the high cost of child care keeps mothers at home, and as families find it difficult financially to live on one salary, the flexibility and income of party sales are appealing.

Most of the agents are women, who say the activity is a way to mix business and pleasure, keeping in touch with the working world while their children are young.

The Baltimore Journal,
5 January 2006.

Looking for words

a. bijoux : ....

b. animal domestique : ....

....

c. travaillant à domicile : ....

....

d. ventes : ....

e. détaillant : ....

f. phénomène : ....

g. actuel : ....

h. lié à : ....

i. garde d'enfants : ....

j. revenu : ....

k. attrayant : ....

l. le monde du travail : ....

Figures

Survival kit, p. 184

a. Complétez les phrases suivantes avec des chiffres du texte.

- More than .... people work in direct-sales units.
- Direct sales represented nearly .... last year.
- Direct selling has been popular in the USA since the ....
- The article was published in January ....

b. Lisez ces phrases à haute voix.

c. Que peut-on dire des mots *million* et *billion* ?

....

d. Comment se traduit en français le "." dans *13.6 million* ?

....

e. Où place-t-on la devise en anglais dans une somme d'argent ?

....

f. Traduisez en anglais : 200 livres sterling, 50 euros, 100 dollars.

....

Document 1 **Practice**

PREMIÈRE PARTIE : REPÉRAGE DE COMPRÉHENSION

1 Exprimez l'idée générale de ce document en français

2 Analysez le titre et le premier paragraphe (l. 1 à 6)

Survival kit, p. 167

a. Le titre est-il explicite ?
b. Repérez un nom propre dans le titre.
c. Qu'apporte le premier paragraphe par rapport au titre ? À quelles questions en *Wh-* répond-il ?

3 Repérez dans le texte

a. Le pays.
b. La forme de commerce.
c. L'effectif des vendeurs et leur sexe.
d. L'horaire pratiqué par la plupart des vendeurs.
e. Le chiffre d'affaires du secteur l'an dernier.
f. Le nom du détaillant qui développe la vente à domicile, en plus de la vente en magasin.
g. Le nom des entreprises sur le marché dans les années 1950.
h. Le type d'articles vendus alors.

4 Vérifiez que vous avez compris

a. Quelle forme de commerce est en plein essor aux États-Unis ?
b. Quels types de produits sont vendus dans ces réunions ?
c. Qui sont les vendeurs ?
d. Quel est l'avantage pour les entreprises de faire vendre leurs produits à domicile ?
e. Quels facteurs expliquent le succès de la vente à domicile ?
f. Qu'apprécient les agents dans cette forme de travail ?

DEUXIÈME PARTIE : REPÉRAGE DE LANGUE

1 L'emploi des formes verbales

Soulignez les verbes dans les phrases suivantes et expliquez leur emploi.

a. The high cost of child care keeps mothers at home.

....

....

b. Sales represented $30 billion last year.

....

....

c. Direct selling has been popular in the USA since the 1950s.

....

....

d. Food gadgets clothing and toys are now being sold at home.

....

....

❷ L'ordre des mots dans les phrases interrogatives

L'ordre des mots dans une question est : auxiliaire + sujet + verbe, sauf quand le pronom interrogatif en *Wh-* est sujet de la phrase.

a. Analysez l'exemple ci-dessous.

Avon Ladies (1) sold beauty products (2) at American homes (3) in the 1950s (4).

1. Who sold beauty products at American homes in the 1950s?
2. What did Avon ladies sell at American homes in the 1950s?
3. Where did Avon ladies sell beauty products in the 1950s?
4. When did the American ladies sell beauty products at American homes?

b. Formulez les questions adéquates pour chacune des phrases suivantes.

Sales (1) represent billions of dollars (2) every year (3) in the USA (4).

1. ....
2. ....
3. ....
4. ....

Women (1) are taking the activity (2) because it is a way to mix business and pleasure (3).

1. ....
2. ....
3. ....

❸ Traduction en anglais

a. La vente directe est populaire aux États-Unis depuis les années 1950.

....

b. La plupart des agents sont des femmes qui souhaitent travailler à temps partiel pendant que leurs enfants sont jeunes.

....

....

c. Les produits Body Shop vendus à domicile sont les mêmes que ceux vendus dans les magasins.

....

....

TROISIÈME PARTIE : AQUISITION DE MÉTHODES

❶ Entraînez-vous au compte rendu oral en anglais

▶ Survival kit, p. 171

a. Préparez l'introduction (sources, idée générale du document) en répondant aux questions en *Wh-* en une phrase.

b. Faites un plan du texte.
1. Facts (Who? Does what? Where?)
2. Reasons for the success of direct sales (Why?)

c. Préparez la conclusion.

❷ Branching out

a. Is direct selling as developed in France as it is in the USA? Why not?

b. Would you like to work from home? Justify your answer.

Document 2

Success for small convenience stores in Japan

Wal-Mart is, no doubt, the world's biggest retailer and the n°1 discount chain in the USA, chain-stores like Tesco and Carrefour are the rising powers in Europe and in Eastern Europe. But, Japan, as usual, is a little different.

One of the hottest retail trends there is the 100 Yen shop, an echo of the dollar stores of the past in the USA.

These stores are designed to appeal to a growing population of money-conscious housewives and older citizens in the world's most rapidly aging nation, and yet they are not discount stores at all.

They are cheap because they sell very small portions. Their best-selling item is the 100 Yen portion of fresh vegetables or fruit, perishable commodities which convenience stores did not offer before.

Most of the 100 Yen shops are located in central cities, they take up no more than 180 square meters, and stay open 16 to 24 hours a day.

Of course, Japan is still one of the leading markets for luxury products but what's happening is that often, nowadays, consumers save on basic goods that are not visible to others, in order to spend more on upmarket brands.

The Washington Journal, 4 August 2006.

retailer: détaillant
hot: à la dernière mode
100 Yen: 0,65 €
to appeal to: attirer
money-conscious: économe
housewife: femme au foyer
item: article
commodity: produit de base
convenience store: magasin de proximité
to save: économiser
upmarket: haut de gamme
brand: marque

Document 3

Growing pains for Wal-Mart

After increasing sales over the fast 40 years, Wal-Mart, the world's biggest retailer, now finds it has to work harder to grow.

In a world where most Americans already live close to a Wal-Mart, it is the company's strategy, and not new retail outlets that will bring higher profits. The company, which operates 3,900 stores in the USA, is under pressure.

Since last year, Wal-Mart has been stocking its stores with trendier women's fashions and higher-end home electronics. The company is also renovating 1,800 stores, widening aisles, lowering shelves, renovating floors and cleaning restrooms. The aim is not to get new customers into the stores but to attract those who come for groceries to the aisles which offer fancier goods.

While Wal-Mart is trying to improve its profile among more affluent shoppers, it also has to improve its corporate image as it faces dozens of lawsuits alleging illegal treatment of its workers and pay discrimination against female employees.

The Arkansas Daily, 19 June 2006.

pain: douleur
outlet/store: magasin
trendy: à la mode
high end: haut de gamme
to widen: élargir
aisle: allée de circulation
to lower: baisser
shelf: rayon
floor: sol
restroom: toilettes
aim: objectif
customer/shopper: client
fancy: chic
affluent: à l'aise financièrement
corporate image: image d'entreprise
lawsuit: action en justice
to allege: alléguer

Présentez ces deux textes à l'oral.

Survival kit, p. 171

Document 4

Biggest shopping centres press for end to Sunday restrictions

Britain's biggest shopping centres are to campaign for an extension in Sunday trading hours.

Managers from malls including Bluewater in Kent, Lakeside in Essex and the Metro Centre in Gateshead* will meet in Manchester today to discuss how to persuade the government to relax the rules that restrict Sunday opening to six hours.

Ron Woodman, general manager of the Metro Centre, which has 380 retailers, said: "Sunday is now the second most popular shopping day after Saturday and although it is up to the individual stores whether they choose to open, profits are such that 99 per cent choose to do so. [...]"

The move will anger religious campaigners and shop workers' unions who vigorously opposed the change in the law in 1994 that finally allowed big stores to trade on Sunday if they accepted limits.

Dr Michael Schluter, director of the Keep Sunday Special Campaign, said: "Most people who work in shops are poorly qualified and not in a position to refuse to work on a Sunday even if they don't want to for fear of getting sacked." [...]

But yesterday, shoppers at Bluewater near Dartford, Britain's biggest shopping centre, seemed in favour of longer shopping hours.

Graham Hudson, a teacher from Streatham, south London, said: "For many people, Sunday is one of the only times they get to shop and it's very inconvenient that you can't start earlier than 11 or later than five."

Christine Pettifer, a housewife from Cann, Dorset, said: "I'm sure the vast majority of people would like to be able to shop whenever they like."

The Home Office said there were no plans to review the issue.

Amanda Kelly,
The Independent, 31 July 2000.
BTS Action commerciale, session 2001.

* The Metro Centre is located in Gateshead (near Newcastle upon Tyne).

Looking for words

a. centre commercial : ....

b. heures d'ouverture : ....

c. directeur : ....

d. assouplir : ....

e. règlements : ....

f. détaillant : ....

g. courses/emplettes : ....

h. magasin : ....

i. bénéfices : ....

j. mettre en colère : ....

k. militant religieux : ....

l. syndicat : ....

m. employé de magasin : ....

n. loi : ....

o. commercer : ....

p. être licencié : ....

q. pas pratique : ....

r. femme au foyer : ....

s. faire des courses : ....

t. ministère de l'Intérieur : ....

u. reconsidérer : ....

v. problème : ....

Document 4 **Practice**

PREMIÈRE PARTIE : REPÉRAGE DE COMPRÉHENSION

1 Exprimez l'idée générale de ce document en français

2 Analysez le titre et le premier paragraphe (l. 1 à 4)

▶ Survival kit, p. 167

a. Quels sont les mots-clés du titre ?
b. Quels mots retrouve-t-on inchangés dans le premier paragraphe ?
c. Quels mots expriment la même idée, différemment ?
d. Quelle précision est ajoutée dans le paragraphe ?

3 Repérez dans le texte

a. Les heures d'ouverture le dimanche des centres commerciaux en Grande-Bretagne.
b. La date de la loi qui a permis l'ouverture des magasins le dimanche.
c. Les jours où les clients sont les plus nombreux dans les centres commerciaux.
d. La ville où les directeurs des centres commerciaux vont se rencontrer.
e. Le nombre de détaillants installés au Metro Centre près de Newcastle upon Tyne.

4 Vérifiez que vous avez compris

a. Pourquoi les directeurs de centres commerciaux vont-ils se rencontrer à Manchester ?
b. La décision d'ouvrir plus longtemps sera-t-elle imposée aux détaillants ? Sera-t-elle bien accueillie, selon le directeur du Metro Centre ? Pourquoi ?
c. Qui est contre ? Pourquoi ?
d. Qui est pour ? Pourquoi ?
e. Comment a réagi le ministère de l'Intérieur britannique ?

DEUXIÈME PARTIE : REPÉRAGE DE LANGUE ET DE CIVILISATION

1 La réutilisation des mots du texte

Complétez les phrases suivantes avec des mots du texte.

– The managers of the .... British shopping .... would like an extension of Sunday .... hours.

– Sunday is the second most popular .... day for the 380 Metro Centre ....

– Workers' .... and religious .... are opposed to a change.

– Most people who work in shops are poorly .... and will have to accept to work on Sundays .... of being ....

– A vast majority of people are in .... of .... shopping .... They think it is very .... not to be able to shop .... they like.

2 Les contraires

À partir des mots du texte, trouvez des contraires pour les expressions suivantes.

– small: ....

– beginning: ....

4

- to limit: ....
- closing: ....
- night: ....
- general: ....
- losses: ....
- to be hired: ....
- shorter: ....
- convenient: ....
- minority: ....

❸ L'emploi des formes verbales

Complétez les phrases suivantes avec les verbes entre parenthèses à la forme qui, selon vous, convient dans le contexte, puis expliquez votre choix.

- The managers of big shopping centres .... today to discuss trading hours. (meet)

....

- In 1994, a law .... big stores to trade on Sundays. (allow)

....

- Big shopping centres .... in England on Sundays from 11am to 5pm since 1994. (be open)

....

- If stores .... longer hours, people .... more easily. (open/come)

....

❹ Le style direct et le style indirect

a. Transformez les phrases suivantes au style indirect.

- L. 15 : Ron Woodman said: "Sunday is the second most popular shopping day after Saturday."

....

....

- L. 36 : Dr Michael Schulter said: "Most people who work in shops are poorly qualified."

....

....

- L. 53 : Graham Hudson said: "Sunday is one of the only times people get to shop and it's very inconvenient that you can't start earlier than 11am."

....

....

....

b. Transformez la phrase suivante au style direct.

- L. 68 : The Home Office said there were no plans to review the issue.

....

....

c. Que remarquez-vous concernant la concordance des temps ?

....

....

❺ Les comparatifs de supériorité et les superlatifs

a. Relevez deux phrases comportant un superlatif et soulignez les adjectifs.

– ....

....

– ....

....

b. Écrivez les adjectifs à la forme simple.

....

c. Comment forme-t-on le superlatif des adjectifs courts et des adjectifs longs ?

....

d. Relevez deux phrases au comparatif de supériorité et soulignez les adjectifs.

– ....

– ....

e. Écrivez les adjectifs à la forme simple.

....

f. Comment forme-t-on le comparatif de supériorité des adjectifs courts ?

....

g. Quelle préposition suit la forme comparative ?

....

❻ Les pronoms relatifs

a. Observez les phrases suivantes :
- Ron Woodman, general manager of the Metro Centre, which has 380 retailers, said…
- The unions who opposed the law…
- The law that allowed stores to open on Sundays…
- Most people who work…

b. Relevez les pronoms relatifs et expliquez leur emploi.

– ....

– ....

– ....

– ....

c. Connaissez-vous d'autres pronoms relatifs ? Lesquels ?

....

❼ La traduction de « pour »

Complétez les phrases suivantes avec *to* ou *for*.

The managers of Britain's biggest shopping centres met in Manchester in July 2000 .... discuss how .... be able to open longer on Sundays. They are

4

campaigning .... the end of the 11-to-5 restriction. Unions are fighting .... the protection of workers; shoppers come on Sundays .... have more time. .... them, the 11-to-5 restriction is inconvenient.

❽ Traduction en anglais

a. Les centres commerciaux anglais sont ouverts le dimanche de 11 heures à 17 heures.

....

....

b. Le Metro Centre, qui a ouvert au milieu des années 1980, est le plus grand centre commercial d'Angleterre.

....

....

c. Les clients qui viennent à Gateshead le dimanche aimeraient arriver plus tôt et partir plus tard pour passer plus de temps dans ce centre commercial.

....

....

d. Les syndicats ne sont pas d'accord avec des horaires d'ouverture plus longs.

....

....

e. Les employés devront accepter de travailler le dimanche, de peur d'être licenciés.

....

....

f. Pour beaucoup de gens, les centres commerciaux sont des lieux de loisirs qui correspondent à de nouveaux besoins.

....

....

❾ Civilisation

▶ Survival kit, p. 186

Où sont situés les centres commerciaux mentionnés dans l'article ?

....

....

....

TROISIÈME PARTIE : ACQUISITION DE MÉTHODES

❶ Préparez un résumé en français

▶ Survival kit, p. 173

a. Relisez l'article en relevant les idées-clés dans chaque paragraphe. Faites ce travail dans l'ordre chronologique. Éliminez ce qui ne vous semble pas important.

b. Rédigez le résumé en introduisant des mots de liaison pour articuler les idées (140 mots environ).

❷ Branching out

a. Log on to the Metro Centre web-site (www.metrocentre-gateshead.co.uk). Download the information and make a presentation in English on the following topic: "Europe's largest shopping and leisure centre".

b. Compare opening hours for shopping centres in Britain and in France.

c. Are you in favour of shops opening on Sundays?

Document 5

Corner shops make a comeback as consumers change their habits

After years spent losing business to the relentless spread of out-of-town supermarkets, corner shops are enjoying an unexpected revival, a survey published today shows.

Consumers with little time to go on long shopping sprees are increasingly turning to these independent neighbourhood shops, the retail analysts Mintel say.

Small food retailers saw stronger growth during 1999 and 2000 than supermarkets, with sales up by 7.7 per cent compared to the 7.4 per cent managed by their larger rivals. The key to their popularity is said to be their proximity to residential areas and later opening hours.

Small shops have typically broadened their range of merchandise from food and lottery tickets to include stamps and emergency items and now offer a variety of other services such as photocopying and film processing. They have also begun to provide more fresh food which caters better for the taste of a more health-conscious clientele.

Richard Caines, a Mintel retail consultant, also put their comeback down to the changing habits of shoppers, who are now more likely to supplement one big fortnightly shop from a large supermarket with regular visits to their local convenience stores for "top-up" and "distress" or emergency visits.

Mr Caines said: "These smaller stores are living up to their names and repositioning themselves as neighbourhood stores with a useful role to play for top-up shopping. [...] They are recreating themselves [...] and operating much more in keeping with market demands."

The survey on the shopping habits of 1,000 people also revealed that despite the continued rise in popularity of Tesco, Sainsbury's and Asda, — which are the subject of 59 per cent of all shopping trips — the loyalty card, established by major stores to secure the devotion of customers, is not keeping shoppers faithful to just one store chain.

Only 15 per cent of shoppers display complete fidelity to their one, favourite grocery store. Three out of 10 shoppers use one other store and more than a fifth use two others. Women tend to show less loyalty than men, visiting four or more stores in addition to their main supermarket.

Arifa Akbar,
The Independent, 12 October 2001.

---

to go on a shopping spree: dépenser son argent dans les magasins
to cater for: satisfaire

4

Faites un compte rendu de ce texte à l'oral.

Survival kit, p. 171

Document 6

Tesco in China

Sir Terry Leahy, chief executive of Tesco, has ruled out making a significant acquisition in the United States, but plans to expand in China, where he wants the company to be a major force.

In an interview with the Observer, Sir Terry said: "People have talked about businesses in the US that could be bought, but I don't think they are right for us. We have had researchers in America, but I can tell you that we have no current plans to make an acquisition there."

China is viewed differently. Tesco last year announced a £140m investment by taking a 50% participation in China's Hymall chain [...].

Tesco already has 50 Chinese hypermarkets in partnership with Hymall, with its biggest presence in Shanghai. Now the plan is to extend in the south of the country and in Beijing.

Tesco generates about a fifth of sales from its overseas operations where it has opted to develop slowly and by linking with local partners. It is in 12 countries covering Eastern Europe, Japan, and Turkey. The company would face competition obstacles in the UK if it tried to acquire any of its principal competitors, but there are no monopoly considerations abroad.

Leahy did not elaborate on why the US was off the agenda in the near term, other than say that "the US is a competitive market, it's a challenging place".

His prudence is likely to be welcomed in the City where investors view the US as a potential graveyard for British retailers. But Leahy is interested in moving to India once New Delhi opens up the sector to foreign investment.

The Guardian, January 8, 2006.

BTS MUC, annales 2006.

Looking for words

a. directeur général : ....

b. exclure : ....

c. chercheur : ....

d. en cours : ....

e. partenariat : ....

f. ventes : ....

g. à l'étranger (2 mots) : ....

....

h. s'associer avec : ....

i. concurrence : ....

j. concurrent : ....

k. donner plus de détails : ....

....

l. plus à l'ordre du jour : ....

m. à court terme : ....

....

n. compétitif : ....

o. qui représente un défi : ....

....

p. être bienvenu : ....

....

q. la Bourse anglaise : ....

r. considérer : ....

s. cimetière : ....

t. détaillant : ....

u. étranger : ....

Document 6 **Practice**

PART 1: UNDERSTANDING THE TEXT

❶ Give the general idea of the article

❷ Analyse the title

Survival kit, p. 167

a. Who? Where?
b. What information is added in the 1st paragraph?

❸ Find the following information in the article

a. The name of the British retailing chain.
b. Sir Terry Leahy's position in the company.
c. The country where Tesco is abandoning its investments.
d. The country where Tesco wants to be powerful.
e. How much Tesco paid for the 50% participation in China's Hymall chain.
f. The number of stores currently operated by Tesco in China.
g. Where in China Tesco is most present.
h. Where in China Tesco would like to open stores.
i. The percentage of sales generated by Tesco overseas, and the countries where the company has stores.
j. The Asian country where Tesco would like to invest.

❹ Make sure you have understood the article

a. What country is Tesco privileging for its future acquisitions?
b. Why is the USA abandoned?
c. How important is Tesco in China?
d. What Chinese retailing chain is Tesco associated with?
e. What is Tesco's strategy abroad?
f. Why is Tesco privileging investments abroad, and not acquisitions of competitors in the UK?
g. Why are investors in the City (= the Stock Exchange) more favourable to investments for Tesco in China rather than in the USA?

PART 2: ENGLISH LANGUAGE

❶ La dérivation

Complétez les phrases suivantes à l'aide d'un mot formé à partir du verbe donné entre parenthèses.

– Tesco's .... in China last year represented £120 million (to invest).

– Tesco has no plans to make .... in the USA (to acquire).

– The company's .... overseas represent 1/5 of sales (to operate).

– .... said the USA was too risky a country for Tesco (to research).

– Monopoly .... imply Tesco would be too powerful if it bought another retailing chain in the UK (to consider).

❷ Les dérivés de *to compete*

a. Cherchez dans le dictionnaire le sens des mots suivants : *competition*, *competitor*, *competitive* (2 sens), *to compete*.

4

b. Complétez le texte avec l'un des mots donnés dans la question précédente :

Tesco has decided to invest in foreign countries because there is too much .... in the UK. The retailer's main .... on the British market are Sainsbury's, Asda and Marks & Spencer. To remain ...., companies offer lower prices or more services to their customers. They also .... on what they do to protect the environment.

❸ La proposition infinitive avec *want*

a. Observez la phrase suivante :
Sir Terry Leahy wants the company to be powerful in China.

b. Quel est le sujet de la proposition principale ?

....

....

c. Quel est le verbe de cette proposition ?

....

....

d. Quel est le verbe de la proposition complément ?

....

....

e. Quel est le sujet de ce verbe et quelle est sa nature ?

....

....

La construction de *want* est toujours identique : *to want* + complément + verbe à l'infinitif.
Se construisent de la même manière les verbes qui expriment une volonté, un ordre, une invitation à faire quelque chose, ou le fait de rendre une action possible (= demander à quelqu'un de...) : *to want, to ask, to tell, to expect, to beg, to remind, to force, to order, to invite, to persuade, to get, to advise, to recommend, to encourage, to permit, to forbid.*

❹ La concordance des temps

a. Observez les temps dans le paragraphe ci-dessous au style direct (l. 11 à l. 20).
Sir Terry said: "People have talked about businesses in the US that could be bought, but I don't think they are right for us. We have had researchers in America, but I can tell you that we have no current plans to make an acquisition there."

b. Transformez le paragraphe au style indirect.

....

....

....

....

....

c. Que remarquez-vous concernant la concordance des temps ?

....

....

....

....

....

❺ Les subordonnées introduites par *if*

a. Observez la phrase suivante relevée dans l'article (l. 41-45) :
The company would face competition obstacles in the UK if it tried to acquire any of its competitors.

b. Soulignez les verbes dans la proposition principale et dans la subordonnée commençant par *if* et indiquez quels sont les formes verbales employées.

....

....

c. Complétez la phrase en exprimant un futur dans la principale.

....

....

d. Complétez la phrase en employant un conditionnel passé dans la principale.

....

....

e. Que remarquez-vous concernant la concordance des temps ?

....

....

f. Traduisez les phrases a, c et d.

....

....

....

....

....

....

g. Que remarquez-vous concernant les verbes employés en français et en anglais ?

....

....

....

❻ Traduction en anglais

a. Tesco réussira en Chine si l'entreprise s'adapte aux consommateurs chinois.

....

....

....

b. L'entreprise aurait des problèmes si elle achetait un concurrent britannique.

....

....

....

c. Tesco n'aurait pas investi 120 millions de livres sterling en Chine si l'entreprise ne s'était pas associée avec des partenaires locaux.

....

....

....

d. Les investisseurs aimeraient que Tesco réussisse en Chine.

....

....

....

e. Sir Terry Leahy demande au gouvernement indien d'ouvrir la distribution aux investissements étrangers.

....

....

....

PART 3: PRACTISING FOR THE EXAM

❶ Faites un compte rendu oral du texte

▶ Survival kit, p. 171

a. Préparez l'introduction (sources, idée générale du document) en répondant aux questions en *Wh-* en une phrase.

b. Faites un plan du texte.
1. Facts
   a) Tesco abroad
   b) Tesco's new strategy
2. Reasons for Tesco's strategy
3. Prospective reaction of the Stock Exchange

c. Préparez la conclusion.

❷ Rédigez un résumé du texte en français en 150 mots (+/– 10 %)

▶ Survival kit, p. 173

❸ Branching out

a. Who are Tesco's 'principal competitors' in the UK? In the world?

b. Find information on the Internet on Wikipedia, the free encyclopedia (http://en.wikipedia.org) on the following hypermarket chains: Tesco, Walmart, Carrefour, and compare them (number of stores on the domestic market and overseas, headquarters, number of employees, website, net income).

c. Prepare your CV and an application letter for work experience at Tesco's London headquarters (www.Tesco.com).
Contact: Mary Britton, Human Resource Manager

▶ Survival kit, pp. 176-177

d. Get ready for an interview with Ms Britton.

Document 7

A Vast Landscape of Malls for China's New Shoppers

DONGGUAN*, China – After construction workers finish plastering a replica of the Arc de Triomphe and buffing the imitation streets of Hollywood, Paris, and Amsterdam, a giant new shopping theme park will proclaim itself the world's largest shopping mall.

The South China Mall – a jumble of Disneyland and Las Vegas – will be nearly three times the size of the vast Mall of America in Minnesota.

Not so long ago, shopping in China consisted mostly of lining up to persuade surly clerks to accept cash in exchange for ugly merchandise that did not fit. But the Chinese have started to embrace America's frenzied "shop till you drop" ethos and are in the midst of a buy-at-the-mall frenzy.

Already, four shopping malls in China are larger than the Mall of America. By 2010, China is expected to have at least 7 of the world's 10 largest malls.

Chinese consumers arrive by bus and train, and growing numbers by car. On busy days, a mall in the southern city of Guangzhou draws about 600,000 shoppers.

China is still a land of disparity, though it has a growing middle class that now numbers about 70 million.

Retail sales in China have jumped nearly 50 per cent in the last four years, as measured by the nation's biggest retailers, while income per person has risen to about $1,100 a year, up 50 per cent since 2000.

"Forget the idea that consumers in China don't have enough money to spend," said David Hand, a real estate and retailing expert at Jones Lang Lasalle in Beijing. "There are people with a lot of money here. And that's driving the development of these shopping malls."

While peasants and poor workers may only browse, the pilgrimage to the mall has builders and developers spending billions of dollars to create supersize shopping centers in the country's fastest-growing cities. [...]

In Dongguan, the South China Mall is a $400 million fantasy land: 60 hectares of palm-tree-lined plazas, theme parks, hotels, water fountains, pyramids, bridges and giant windmills.

The New York Times, extraits, David Barbeza, June 4, 2005.
BTS Assistant de direction, session 2006.

* Dongguan is an industrial city located near Hong Kong in Southern China.

to buff: fignoler
jumble: mélange
to line up: faire la queue
surly: revêche
clerk: employé
to fit: être de la bonne taille
frenzy: frénésie
to drop: tomber (de fatigue)
ethos: philosophie
income: revenu
real estate: immobilier
peasant: paysan
to browse: regarder
pilgrimage: pèlerinage
windmill: moulin à vent

Faites un compte rendu de ce texte à l'oral.

Survival kit, p. 171

Document 8

La mutation des grands magasins de centre-ville

[...] « *Tout a commencé avec la guerre du Golfe*, explique Jacques Périllat, directeur général de l'UCV (Union du commerce de centre-ville). *Les grands magasins, confrontés à de vraies difficultés, se sont demandé s'ils ne devaient pas transformer leur offre.* » À cette époque, les hypermarchés se développaient en périphérie et s'emparaient du marché de l'alimentaire.

Autour d'eux, les Castorama et autres Leroy Merlin attiraient les bricoleurs. Dans le même temps, les centres-villes étaient désertés par les habitants qui s'installaient en banlieue. « *Il a fallu convaincre les pouvoirs publics de favoriser le centre-ville en améliorant la circulation, la sécurité, les parkings et en ramenant des logements* », poursuit Jacques Périllat.

Les grands magasins ont réagi en effectuant une véritable mutation. « *Le concept de magasin populaire d'il y a quinze ans est dépassé*, constate Philippe Houzé, coprésident du directoire des Galeries Lafayette. *Aujourd'hui, les magasins doivent être des vaisseaux amiraux, exerçant une attractivité importante sur les clients avec des produits de mode et des marques. L'offre doit être tirée vers le haut de gamme.* »

Première règle d'or, la consommation de masse s'étant déplacée en périphérie, le commerce de centre-ville s'est concentré sur les produits de qualité, plus sophistiqués. Cette évolution a été accélérée par la forte progression du pouvoir d'achat des cadres ces dernières années.

Ainsi, les magasins qui, dans les années 1990, mettaient en avant leurs marques propres – très profitables compte tenu de leurs fortes marges – ont changé leur fusil d'épaule et se sont concentrés sur les marques reconnues, plus prestigieuses. Désormais, le Printemps réalise 85 % de son chiffre d'affaires avec des marques, Au Bon Marché jusqu'à 95 %.

Dans le même temps, tous se sont concentrés sur leurs points forts. Le Printemps a abandonné ses rayons loisirs, disques, électroménager et bricolage. « *Notre stratégie n'est pas d'avoir tout, mais tout ce qu'il faut par univers, avec un certain parti pris* », explique Laurence Danon, présidente du directoire du Printemps. [...]

À Paris, chacun s'est adapté à la clientèle de son quartier. Boulevard Haussmann, les acheteurs sont à 30 % à 40 % des touristes et des étrangers (plus encore pour les Galeries Lafayette), les autres se partageant entre des habitants des VIIIe, IXe, XVIe arrondissements et de la banlieue ouest qui prennent leur train gare Saint-Lazare. De plus, la moyenne d'âge a baissé, passant de 45 ans en 1995 à 35 ans aujourd'hui. Il fallait donc moderniser l'offre. [...]

Cette mutation a un coût. Depuis quatre ans, le Printemps a investi 182,94 millions d'euros pour moderniser ses magasins et les Galeries Lafayette 167,69 millions d'euros.

Pierre Avril,
Le Figaro Économie,
17 octobre 2001.

Questions

1. Make a list of the French stores mentioned in the article and differentiate their activities.

2. Why did department stores start thinking about a new strategy?

3. Explain the current change in French department stores as regards:
a. the offer,
b. the customers targeted,
c. the cost of the change.

Chapter 5.
The environment

Document 1

Water problems for Coca Cola in India

The world's biggest drinks firm is being targeted by green activists in India over the issue of water.

Coca Cola is accused of aggravating the growing global problem of fresh-water insufficiency, as experts from New Delhi's Centre for Science and Environment say some of the firm's bottling plants use too much water in drought-prone areas, to the detriment of poor local villagers.

Company officials argue the company operates in 200 countries, and started controlling the use of water long before the problems in India. They say they have improved their water efficiency by 6%, reducing the volume of water needed to clean assembly lines and wash out glass bottles from 3.12 litres in 2002 to 2.72 litres in 2004.

But Indian environmentalists are not impressed. They say they do not understand how a firm that calls itself a "hydration company" can waste so much water.

To improve the situation, Coca Cola has just completed a detailed estimation of "water risks" in India, going plant by plant, calculating water needs and consequences for local communities.

Coca Cola is also working with non-governmental groups such as WWF and CARE so as to improve its corporate image.

The British Journal, 6 June 2006.

Looking for words

a. prendre pour cible/viser : ....

b. écologiste : ....

c. à propos de : ....

d. mondial : ....

e. eau douce : ....

f. mise en bouteille : ....

g. usine : ....

h. sujet à la sécheresse : ....

i. soutenir : ....

j. améliorer : ....

k. nettoyer : ....

l. chaîne de montage : ....

m. gâcher : ....

n. ONG : ....

Figures

1. Écoutez, écrivez et lisez à haute voix les chiffres que vous repérez.

a. Deux dates : ....

b. Une centaine : ....

c. Un pourcentage : ....

d. Deux chiffres : ....

À quoi correspondent les « . » en anglais ?

2. Entraînez-vous à dire la date de publication de l'article de deux manières différentes.

Document 1 **Practice**

PREMIÈRE PARTIE : REPÉRAGE DE COMPRÉHENSION

1 Exprimez l'idée générale de ce document en français

2 Analysez le titre et le premier paragraphe

Survival kit, p. 167

a. Repérez les réponses aux *Wh-* questions dans le titre : *What? For whom? Where?*

b. Qu'apporte le premier paragraphe par rapport au titre ?

3 Repérez dans le texte

a. Le nom de l'entreprise concernée.

b. Le nombre de pays dans le monde où l'entreprise est implantée.

c. Le pays concerné.

d. Le nom de la capitale.

e. L'objet du litige.

f. L'enjeu.

g. Le pourcentage d'amélioration apporté par Coca-Cola dans son utilisation de l'eau entre 2002 et 2004.

h. Le nom des ONG avec lesquelles l'entreprise travaille pour améliorer son image.

4 Vérifiez que vous avez compris

a. Qui accuse Coca-Cola ?

b. De quoi l'entreprise est-elle accusée ?

c. Comment se défend-elle ?

d. Les écologistes indiens sont-ils convaincus par ces arguments ?

e. Quelle analyse l'entreprise vient-elle de terminer en Inde pour améliorer la situation ?

f. Que fait également Coca-Cola pour améliorer son image ?

DEUXIÈME PARTIE : REPÉRAGE DE LANGUE

1 L'emploi des formes verbales

a. Relevez les phrases du texte qui citent les propos des différents acteurs.

L. 6 : Experts: ....

L. 12 : Company officials: ....

L. 21 : Indian environmentalists: ....

b. À quelle forme sont les verbes ? Pourquoi ?

....

c. Repérez un verbe au prétérit et expliquez son emploi.

L. 13 : they ....

d. Repérez un *present perfect* et expliquez son emploi.

L. 25-26 : Coca-Cola ....

2 La forme passive

a. Relevez deux phrases à la forme passive (l. 1 et l. 4).

....

....

b. Soulignez le verbe dans chacune des deux phrases.

c. Comment forme-t-on le passif ?

....

d. Pourquoi le premier verbe au passif est-il suivi d'un complément d'agent et l'autre pas ?

....

❸ L'emploi des prépositions

En vous reportant au texte si nécessaire, complétez les phrases avec les prépositions suivantes : *of* – *in* – *by* – *for* – *to* – *among* – *with* – *of* – *over*. Attention, certaines peuvent être utilisées plusieurs fois, et d'autres pas du tout.

Coca Cola is facing problems .... image .... India. It is being targeted .... green activists .... the problem .... water. It is accused .... aggravating the problem .... fresh water .... the world, ... wasting too much water .... its bottling plants, ... regions where there are often droughts. .... improve the situation .... the environmentalists, and because it wants to keep a good corporate image .... its customers, Coca Cola has just carried out an estimation .... water needs .... local Indian communities.

❹ Traduction en anglais

a. L'entreprise Coca-Cola est accusée d'aggraver le problème de l'eau douce dans le monde, car elle utilise trop d'eau dans ses usines d'embouteillage.

....

....

b. Les responsables de l'entreprise disent qu'ils ont réduit le volume d'eau nécessaire pour nettoyer les bouteilles.

....

....

c. Les écologistes indiens ne comprennent pas comment Coca-Cola peut gaspiller autant d'eau, au détriment de la population locale.

....

....

TROISIÈME PARTIE : AQUISITION DE MÉTHODES

❶ Entraînez-vous au compte rendu oral en anglais

a. Préparez l'introduction (sources, idée générale du document) en répondant aux questions en *Wh-* en une phrase.

b. Faites un plan du texte.
1. Facts (Who? Does what? Against whom? Why?)
2. Reactions of the company

c. Préparez la conclusion.

❷ Branching out

Connectez-vous sur Internet et cherchez des informations sur Coca-Cola (actions d'entreprise citoyenne), sur le WWF et sur CARE.

Document 2

The big chains all want to be green grocers

For years, the supermarkets have been fighting on price, but recently, they have found a new battleground: the protection of the environment.

Last week, Tesco unveiled a 10-point plan to present itself as the "good neighbour" store, caring for the community. Items in the plan ranged from sponsoring mass running and walking events to erecting wind turbines on store roofs.

Yesterday, Sainsbury's CEO Justin King announced new compostable bags, made from a protein, were being tested for Sainsbury's organic fruit and vegetables.

Last year, Asda and its Walmart parent made a $550 million commitment to a range of long-term environment goals. It promised the chain would be supplied 100% by renewable energy, it would create zero waste, reduce greenhouse emissions and cut dependence on oil.

This year, Mr Lee Scott, Walmart's president, obtained a two-hour audience with Prince Charles to get royal advice on how to become more ecologically sound.

Chief executive Sir Terry Leahy insists that Tesco's initiative simply mirrors changes in society. He says consumers are increasingly concerned about the environment. To keep them as loyal customers, the company must innovate to meet their changing needs. "We have a wider responsibility to society," the CEO says.

Adapted from *The Guardian*, 18 May 2006.

battleground: champ de bataille
item: article
wind turbine: éolienne
organic: biologique
parent: maison mère
waste: déchet
greenhouse: à effet de serre
oil: pétrole
advice: conseils
sound: valable, sérieux
loyal: fidèle

Document 3

Global warming seen pushing up insurance costs

Global warming will push up insurance premiums in high-risk areas like coastal Florida and other hurricane-prone parts of the United States, an insurance company official said on Tuesday.

"That it will cost more, there's no question; we can put that on the table right at the beginning," said Clem Booth, a board member of Allianz Group. […]

Other likely consequences of global warming, including an increase in wildfires in the American West, will also need to be taken into account by U.S. insurers, according to a report by Allianz and conservation group World Wildlife Fund. […]

Currently, Booth said, insurers withdraw from these high-risk areas entirely.

"This report and other reports are making it clear that there is a direct correlation between climate change, forest fires, storm surges and people livelihoods," said Carter Roberts, president of WWF in the United States. "I think right now the U.S. public is waking up to just what an enormous risk this represents for them."

Booth said the disastrous 2005 U.S. hurricane season, especially the costly destruction of Hurricane Katrina, was a wake-up for U.S. insurers. […]

Insurers need to work with government to make sure construction in those areas dealt with the risk and did not continue "business as usual".

AlertNet News Reuters Foundation, 10 October 2006.

premium: prime (d'assurance)
hurricane: ouragan
prone to: prédisposé à
board: conseil d'administration
wildfire: feu de forêt
to withdraw: se retirer
storm: tempête
surge: déchaînement
livelihood: moyen d'existence
to wake up to: prendre conscience
to deal with: prendre en compte

Présentez ces deux textes à l'oral.

Survival kit, p. 171

5

Document 4

Prince's organic food profits triple

ORGANIC FARMING is bringing home the bacon for the Prince of Wales. Duchy Originals, his organic-food company, increased its profits almost threefold last year as sales of organic food soared.

The green-minded royal now owns the country's leading independent organic-food brand. [...]

Belinda Gooding, managing director, said the rise stemmed from the growing interest in organic food and the success of the Duchy's pork products.

Duchy Originals' profits rose to £502,806 last year from £177,841 the previous year, according to accounts filed last month. About £400,000 of the profit was paid to the Prince of Wales's Charitable Foundation.

The company, now chaired by Guy McCracken, a former Marks & Spencer director, was launched 11 years ago, selling biscuits made with organic wheat from the Prince's Highgrove estate.

Gooding said Prince Charles had given the brand integrity at a time when cynicism about organic food was growing. "People know he is passionate about organic farming and the integrity of his products comes first," she said.

Last year's most successful products were Duchy bacon and sausages and Lemon Refresher, a soft drink aimed at adults. Nielsen, the ratings agency, says Refresher is the fastest growing in its market.

Gooding said the company would be launching a range of chocolate biscuits and bread products this year. She said Prince Charles often contributed ideas for new products and had helped develop the pork range.

The value of the organic-food market grew 40% last year after a 40% rise the year before, according to Mintel. About 70% of baby food sold is now organic. Waitrose was the first grocer to stock Duchy Originals. The Prince's goods are now sold by most big chains.

Steven Easom, buying director at Waitrose, said: "Organic food has become part of the weekly shopping basket. When people think about food now they are also thinking about where it came from and how it was made."

The Sunday Times, January 7, 2001.

organic food: produits biologiques
to soar: monter en flèche
to stem from: avoir pour origine

Duchy Originals in 2005

– 130 products are sold: biscuits, natural hair care products, sausages and bacon, ale, crisps, chutneys, mustard and milk

– Profits in 2004: £1 million, donated to Prince Charles' Charitable Foundation.

Looking for words

a. agriculture biologique : ....

b. lard : ....

c. pays de Galles : ....

d. bénéfices : ....

e. ventes : ....

f. écologiste : ....

g. n° 1 : ....

h. marque : ....

i. directeur/-trice : ....

j. classer : ....

k. présider : ....

l. créer : ....

m. blé : ....

n. saucisses : ....

o. citron : ....

p. gamme : ....

q. épicier : ....

r. référencer : ....

Document 4 Practice

PREMIÈRE PARTIE : REPÉRAGE DE COMPRÉHENSION

1 Exprimez l'idée générale de ce document en français

2 Analysez le titre et le premier paragraphe (l. 1 à 7) Survival kit, p. 167

a. Quels sont les mots-clés du titre ?
b. Où se trouve le verbe dans le titre ?
c. Où est le sujet dans le titre ?
d. Qu'apporte le premier paragraphe ?

3 Repérez dans le texte

a. Le nom de l'entreprise et sa date de création.
b. Le nom du propriétaire.
c. Le nom du président.
d. Le nom de la directrice générale.
e. La progression des bénéfices de l'entreprise entre 1999 et 2000.
f. La position de l'entreprise sur le marché bio en Grande-Bretagne.
g. Le pourcentage de croissance du bio en Grande-Bretagne en 1999 et en 2000.
h. Le pourcentage du bio dans les aliments pour bébés.

4 Vérifiez que vous avez compris

a. Quelles sont les raisons du récent succès des produits Duchy Originals ?
b. Depuis quand le prince Charles s'intéresse-t-il aux produits bio ?
c. Que vend son entreprise ?
d. Quels sont ses projets ?
e. Où sont vendus les produits Duchy Originals ?
f. Comment le prince Charles utilise-t-il les bénéfices de l'entreprise ?

DEUXIÈME PARTIE : REPÉRAGE DE LANGUE ET DE CIVILISATION

1 L'utilisation des pronoms relatifs

Complétez le texte suivant avec les pronoms suivants : *when - who - which - how - why - where - that.*

Duchy Originals was launched by Charles .... was passionate about organic farming at a time .... the environment was not as popular an issue as nowadays. Most of the profit .... is made by the company is given to the Prince's charities. One of the reasons .... "Duchy Originals" is popular is .... people now want to know .... their food comes from and .... it was made.

2 L'ordre des mots dans les questions

Organisez les phrases suivantes en questions.

– was / When / launched / Duchy Originals / ?

....

– Who / the / chairman / is / ?

....

5

– does / it / sell / What / ?

....

– the / products / Where / are / sold / ?

....

– Prince / Has / Charles / got / to play / a role / in the firm / ?

....

– reasons / of / company / the / the / the / for / success / What / are / ?

....

❸ La forme passive

a. Relevez les phrases à la forme passive dans le texte.

– L. 20 : ....

....

– L. 25 : ....

....

– L. 57 : ....

....

– L. 65 : ....

....

b. Une seule est suivie d'un complément d'agent. Laquelle ? Pourquoi ?

....

❹ Le style direct et le style indirect

a. Les informations concernant l'entreprise et ses résultats sont rapportées par Belinda Gooding au style indirect. Recopiez les phrases concernées.

– L. 11 : ....

....

– L. 29 : ....

....

– L. 43 : ....

....

b. Écrivez les phrases au style direct en commençant par : *Belinda Gooding said: "…".*

– ....

....

– ....

....

– ....

....

c. Que remarquez-vous ?

....

....

d. Steven Easom, directeur des achats chez Waitrose, parle des produits bio au style direct (l. 59).
Rapportez ses propos au style indirect en commençant la phrase par : *Steven Easom said.*

....

....

e. Que remarquez-vous ?

....

5 Le cas possessif

Le cas possessif, ou « génitif », s'emploie :
– pour exprimer l'appartenance pour un être animé (personne ou animal) ;
– pour désigner quelque chose en relation avec une activité humaine ;
– pour exprimer un moment, une distance, une durée, un lieu.

Relevez dans le texte des expressions utilisant le cas possessif et expliquez leur emploi.

– Dans le titre : ....

....

– L. 9 : ....

....

– L. 15 : ....

....

– L. 21 : ....

....

– L. 28 : ....

....

– L. 36 : ....

....

6 Traduction en anglais

a. L'entreprise Duchy Originals fut fondée par le prince de Galles il y a plus de dix ans, à une époque où le bio n'était pas à la mode.

....

....

b. Maintenant, en raison de l'ESB (ou maladie de la vache folle) et de l'épidémie de fièvre aphteuse en 2001, les consommateurs veulent savoir d'où vient la nourriture qu'ils achètent.

....

....

....

7 Civilisation

▶ Survival kit, p. 187

a. Answer the following questions in English about the British Royal Family and government.
– Why is Prince Charles called the Prince of Wales? (locate Wales an the map p. 188)

....

5

- Who is the current monarch?

....

- What are the British Monarch functions?

....

- Who actually governs the country?

....

- Who is the current Prime Minister? Which political party does he belong to?

....

b. What other "big" grocery chains do you know in Britain?

....

....

....

TROISIÈME PARTIE : ACQUISITION DE MÉTHODES

❶ Traduisez en français les paragraphes 1 et 2 (l. 1 à 10)

▶ Survival kit, p. 174

Attention à la traduction des mots composés.

❷ Jeu de rôles

▶ Survival kit, p. 181

1. Trois étudiants joueront ce jeu de rôles en anglais :
- Belinda Gooding, directrice de l'entreprise Duchy Originals ;
- Steven Easom, directeur des achats chez Waitrose, chaîne de magasins britannique ;
- Jérémie ou Aurélie, stagiaire à Londres chez Euromarket Surveys. Cette entreprise va représenter la Grande-Bretagne au Salon des produits du terroir qui se tiendra au printemps en France.

2. Afin de construire ce jeu de rôles, chaque étudiant devra se constituer une fiche :
- Belinda Gooding sur Duchy Originals ;
- Steven Easom sur le marché bio dans les grandes surfaces ;
- Jérémie ou Aurélie sur le thème suivant : « La percée des produits bio en Grande-Bretagne, un pionnier, le prince Charles, prince de Galles ».

Le ou la stagiaire devra également construire son entretien sur des questions diverses et variées concernant la date de création de l'entreprise, les produits vendus, la position de l'entreprise sur son secteur, la gamme de clientèle, les canaux de distribution, le rôle du prince Charles, les raisons du succès dans la grande distribution et les projets de l'entreprise pour l'avenir.

❸ Branching out

▶ Survival kit, pp. 176-177

Suite à cette étude, vous décidez de postuler pour un stage dans l'entreprise Duchy Originals. Préparez une lettre de motivation à laquelle vous joindrez votre curriculum vitæ.

Contact : Belinda Gooding, Managing Director
Duchy Originals
27 Hyde Park Corner road
LONDON
W1
ROYAUME-UNI

Document 5

Bangalore faces e-waste hazards

A TIME BOMB is ticking in Bangalore, India's hi-tech capital, but most of its six million inhabitants are largely unaware of the threat.

Home to more than 1,200 foreign and domestic technology firms, Bangalore figures prominently in the list of cities faced with e-waste hazard. "The end effects of electronic junk generated from obsolete computers and discarded electronic components are disastrous to our environment and people," says Mr Sreenath acclaimed as an e-waste recycling expert.

[…] Mr Sreenath has set up Asia's first e-waste crematorium, the Indian Computer Crematorium. "Here we neither bury nor burn electronic waste. It is done through a mechanical dry recycling process," he says.

Domestic e-waste including computers, refrigerators, televisions and mobiles contain more than 1,000 different toxic materials which can lead to cancer. Officials say second-hand computers from the West get dumped in India, most of it done illegally by grey market operators.

Hundreds of recyclers of discarded computers and electronic components across India sell second-hand parts to private computer assemblers. They work with their bare hands and are not aware of the health risks. "It is very sad. Most of them are uneducated, we are trying to create awareness," says Mr Screenath.

India's hardware organisation, the Manufacturers Association of Information Technology (MAIT), has persuaded the government in Dehli to set up a federal agency to handle waste disposal.

BBC News, 31 January 2006.
BTS Assistant de direction, session 2006.

hazard: danger
time bomb: bombe à retardement
threat: menace
domestic: national
waste: déchet
to discard/to dump: jeter
dry: à sec
second-hand: d'occasion
bare: nu
awareness: prise de conscience
hardware: matériel informatique

Faites un compte rendu oral de ce texte en anglais.

Survival kit, p. 171

5

Document 6

A tankful of sugar

Has Brazil found the answer to high petrol prices?

While motorists elsewhere worry about high fuel prices, new car buyers in Brazil can feel happy. They can fill up with petrol, ethanol (alcohol) or any combination of the two. And right now, ethanol is up to 55% cheaper at the pump in Brazil than regular gasoline.

Brazilians are the beneficiaries of an automotive revolution: "flex-fuel" cars that run as readily on ethanol as on regular petrol were introduced in 2003, have since grabbed nearly two-thirds of the market. [...]

In Brazil, ethanol is everywhere, thanks to a 30-year-old policy of promoting fuel derived from home-grown sugar cane.

Eager for energy independence or lower emissions of greenhouse gases, other countries are now starting to promote "bio-fuels". But America and Europe favour their own farmers, who produce fuel based on corn or rape-seed that is mainly used as an additive to conventional petrol – and is dirtier and more expensive than Brazil's sugar-based ethanol. So bio-fuelled cars may take years to catch on in other markets [...].

The Brazilian car industry as a whole is struggling. Might exports of flex-fuel cars prove its salvation? Probably not, alas. If the cars become popular outside Brazil, they could easily be made elsewhere [...]. Brazil's biggest opportunity may be to sell fuel rather than flexibility. Its cost of sugar production is so low that ethanol can compete with petrol even with oil prices at $35 a barrel, about half of today's price.

The Economist, 24 September 2005.

BTS CGO et MUC, session 2006.

Looking for words

a. réservoir : ....

b. automobiliste : ....

c. rouler à : ....

d. facilement : ....

e. prendre : ....

f. sur place : ....

g. désireux : ....

h. réduit : ....

i. gaz à effet de serre : ....

j. principalement : ....

k. avoir du succès : ....

l. avoir des problèmes : ....

m. se révéler : ....

n. salut : ....

Looking for words related to energy

a. essence : ....

b. carburant : ....

c. faire le plein : ....

d. éthanol : ....

e. pompe (à essence) : ....

f. à bi-carburant : ....

g. ordinaire : ....

h. canne à sucre : ....

i. biocarburant : ....

j. blé : ....

k. colza : ....

l. à base de sucre : ....

m. pétrole : ....

n. baril : ....

Document 6 Practice

PART 1: UNDERSTANDING THE TEXT

❶ Give the general idea of the article

❷ Analyse the title and the subtitle

Survival kit, p. 167

a. The title
- Is it explicit?
- Try and explain the pun on the word 'tankful'.

b. The subtitle
Answer the *Wh*- questions: who? Has done what?

❸ Find the following information in the article

a. The country where ethanol is used to fill up car tanks.
b. How much cheaper ethanol is compared to regular gasoline.
c. When flex-fuel cars were introduced in Brazil.
d. What part of the market they represent.
e. For how long Brazil has been promoting ethanol, i.e. fuel derived from sugar cane.
f. The price of a barrel of oil in 2005.

❹ Make sure you have understood the article

a. Why are Brazilian motorists happier than motorists elsewhere?
b. What are "flex-fuel" cars?
c. Are they popular in Brazil?
d. Why is ethanol so cheap?
e. When did Brazil promote ethanol as an alternative fuel?
f. Compare Brazilian ethanol and US and European "bio-fuels".
g. What are the drawbacks of bio-fuels compared to Brazilian ethanol?
h. Will Brazil sell "flex-fuel" cars abroad?
i. What could it sell abroad? Why?

PART 2: ENGLISH LANGUAGE

❶ Le vocabulaire pétrolier

Complétez les phrases en choisissant parmi les mots suivants : *flex-fuel – lead-free – fuel – barrel – oil – petrol – gasoline – diesel oil – oil-exporting – oil-shock – regular.*

a. Motorists buy .... or .... at the pump.

b. The price of .... has skyrocketed since the first .... in 1974.

c. A .... of .... cost $70 in 2005.

d. .... cars can run on ethanol or on ..../ ....(2 words).

e. Bio- .... reduce our dependency on .... countries.

f. A lot of cars and trucks in France run on .... because it is cheaper than ....

5

❷ La dérivation

Complétez les phrases suivantes en utilisant pour chaque phrase un mot formé à partir de l'élément donné entre parenthèses.

a. Brazilian .... are happy (motor).

b. The new car .... can purchase "flex-fuel" cars (to buy).

c. They can fill their tanks with ethanol, petrol or a .... of the two (to combine).

d. In Europe, bio-fuel made by .... from corn or rape-seed is used as an additive to .... petrol (farm/convention).

e. The .... of Brazilian ethanol is very .... (to produce/to compete).

❸ Les composés de *-where*

a. Repérez dans le texte deux mots formés avec *where* (l. 1 et l. 14) et traduisez-les.

....

....

....

b. En connaissez-vous d'autres ? Donnez leur traduction.

....

....

....

c. Complétez le paragraphe ci-dessous en réutilisant ces mots.

In Brazil, ethanol can be bought ...., in every petrol station. .... you go, you can see people driving 'flex-cars'. But .... in the world, you cannot use ethanol as an alternative fuel, and you can't find 'flex-fuel' cars .... Such cars are used ....

I'd like to live .... where I could use bio fuel, because it contributes to reduce greenhouse emissions.

❹ L'emploi de deux modaux au présent et au conditionnel

a. Observez les phrases suivantes.

– **Can/could**
L. 3 : *New car buyers in Brazil can feel happy.*
L. 32 : *They could easily be made.*

– **May/might**
L. 25 : *Bio-fuelled cars may take years to catch on in other markets.*
L. 29 : *Might exports of flex-fuel cars prove its salvation?*

b. Soulignez les modaux.

c. Traduisez les phrases suivantes.

– Vous avez peut-être raison, l'éthanol pourrait/risque de devenir le carburant du 21e siècle.

....

....

– Au Brésil, les automobilistes peuvent acheter de l'éthanol à la pompe.

....

....

– En Europe, nous pourrions utiliser le colza si les agriculteurs sont d'accord pour en planter partout.

....

....

5 Les comparatifs de supériorité

Repérez un adjectif au comparatif de supériorité (l. 7) signifiant « meilleur marché » et son contraire (l. 24), signifiant « plus cher ».
Complétez ensuite le tableau ci-dessous.

Adjectif en français	En anglais	Au comparatif	Son contraire	Au comparatif
bon marché				
petit				
bien/bon				
laid				
beaucoup				
sale				
jeune				
difficile				
de bonne heure				
lourd				
intelligent				

6 Les questions comprenant un verbe construit avec une préposition

Utilisez les mots soulignés de chaque phrase pour poser des questions. Ajoutez la préposition avec laquelle le verbe se construit.

a. Motorists in the world worry about <u>high petrol prices</u>.

....

....

b. The Brazilians fill up with <u>petrol, ethanol or any combination of the two</u>.

....

....

....

c. "Flex-fuel" cars run on <u>ethanol or on petrol</u>.

....

....

d. Ethanol is derived from home-grown sugar cane.

....

....

e. Ethanol can compete with petrol.

....

....

PART 3: PRACTISING FOR THE EXAM

❶ Rédigez un compte rendu en français du texte

Survival kit, p. 173

a. Préparez l'introduction.

b. Faites un plan du texte en vous aidant du plan proposé :

1. Développement des biocarburants dans le monde
   a) Les faits
   b) Les raisons du développement
2. Applications
   a) Au Brésil
   b) Aux États-Unis et en Europe
3. Perspectives

c. Préparez la conclusion.

❷ Traduisez en français de "The Brazilian car industry…" (l. 28) jusqu'à "flexibility" (l. 34).

❸ Branching out

a. Why is petrol/gasoline expensive at the pump in Europe? Why is it cheaper in the USA?

b. Why do we need to develop alternative fuels?

c. How can we reduce our dependency to oil?

Document 7

The bugs in the bin that keep watch on your waste

Sitting by the backdoor or at the bottom of the drive, they look inoffensive enough.

But yesterday it was revealed that up to half a million wheelie bins contain a sinister secret – they are fitted with surveillance devices. The bugs, which are a little bigger than a 1 penny piece, are screwed under the lips of wheelie bins and transmit information to sensors on rubbish trucks.

They identify which house a bin belongs to and could one day be used in a 'pay as you throw' system to charge householders by the weight of their rubbish.

In Germany, where the 'Bin Brother' chips are made, families pay 18p per kilo of rubbish that is not recycled. Now, the Local Government Association is calling for a similar system to be introduced in Britain.

Under the scheme, council tax would be cut by approximately £100 – but 'a rubbish tax' would be introduced. Those who recycle would pay less, while families who refuse to sort out their glass, tins, and green waste would be hit with bigger bills. [...]

However critics say the 'chip and bin' system poses a risk to security and civil liberties.

If criminals hack into the data-base, they could find out who is on holiday because they are not putting their bins out. [...]

Rubbish experts said Britain, which has the third-worst recycling record in Europe, has no choice. A typical adult produces 600kg of waste every year [...]. Just 18% is recycled or composted; 8% is incinerated and 78% goes to landfill. [...]

It is estimated that Britain's landfill sites will be full in just eight years' time.

The Daily Mail,
August 28, 2006.

---

drive: allée
wheelie bin: poubelle à roulettes
bug: (ici) mouchard
screwed: vissé
lip: bord
rubbish: ordures
truck: camion
to charge: faire payer
weight: poids
to sort out: trier
bill: facture
to hack into: s'introduire en fraude dans
landfill: décharge

Faites un compte rendu oral de ce texte en anglais.

Survival kit, p. 171

Document 8

Climat : le rapport qui accuse

MÉTÉO. Une hausse planétaire des températures, la Camargue et la Provence menacées par la sécheresse et les inondations, une augmentation des pluies… Un rapport scientifique rendu public confirme les pires inquiétudes sur le réchauffement de la Terre.

L'avenir que nous promet le Giec (groupement intergouvernemental sur l'évolution du climat) dépasse toutes les prévisions que les scientifiques et les politiques nous assénaient depuis quelques années à propos du réchauffement climatique.

Réunie hier à Shanghai, la communauté scientifique internationale du Giec a rendu public un rapport d'un millier de pages rassemblant toutes les données les plus sérieuses récoltées depuis trois ans sur le sujet. Un cri d'alarme, alors que les gouvernements ne parviennent toujours pas à s'entendre sur les moyens de réduire la pollution atmosphérique (effet de serre) à l'origine de ce réchauffement.

Il y a pourtant urgence, car ce rapport annonce, pêle-mêle, la mort des bancs de coraux, l'engloutissement des Maldives ou encore du Bangladesh, la fonte des glaces, la recrudescence de maladies tropicales ou encore la disparition d'espèces animales, comme l'ours polaire. Les prémices ? Jamais siècle ne fut plus chaud, depuis mille ans, que le XXe siècle, et, durant toute cette période, c'est l'année 1998 qui remporte la palme. Depuis près de quarante ans, la couverture neigeuse mondiale s'est rétrécie de 10 %, comme peau de chagrin.

Jusqu'à 6 °C de plus à la fin du siècle

Membre de la mission interministérielle de l'effet de serre (Mies) et, à ce titre, présent à Shanghai, Marc Gillet explique comment on a pu en arriver là : « Nous avons travaillé à partir de 35 scénarios différents, et tous ont montré une accentuation du réchauffement climatique. Pendant des heures, les scientifiques ont discuté pour savoir si l'activité humaine était responsable de ce réchauffement. La réponse est oui. […] »

Les chiffres sont éloquents, on rejette actuellement 370 ppm (parties pour million) de gaz carbonique dans le monde. Ces émissions atteindront 500 à 1 200 ppm à l'horizon 2100. Résultats : le mercure montera de 1,5 à 6 °C, alors qu'au dernier Giec, en 1995, on pensait ne pas dépasser les 4 °C. Le niveau des océans grimpera, lui, de 10 cm à 1 m. Les précipitations, accrues de 2 à 4 % depuis les cinquante dernières années, tomberont de plus belle. […]

Dans une même région, on pourra même assister à des dérèglements climatiques contraires : ainsi, la Provence ou la Camargue sont menacées d'engloutissement, tandis que la disparition des glaciers alpins finira par tarir les rivières et assécher les zones méditerranéennes.

Les États-Unis refusent de moins polluer

Plusieurs mesures existent pour limiter les dégâts : « En premier lieu, faire des économies d'énergie, souligne Marc Gillet. Il est impératif de diminuer l'utilisation d'énergies polluantes comme le pétrole et le charbon. Il faut préférer les transports en commun, le ferroutage, recouvrir les décharges pour éliminer les émanations de méthane, mieux isoler l'habitat. »

Quant à éviter les catastrophes annoncées : « Une meilleure gestion des infrastructures permettra de faire face aux inondations et aux tempêtes. Des digues, par exemple, mais aussi le comblement de la mer en bordure du littoral devraient pouvoir freiner les vents violents. » […]

Jacqueline Meillon,
Le Parisien, 22 janvier 2001.

Questions

1. What are the reasons for global warming?

2. What is consequently changing in our environment?

3. What are the forecasts?

4. What are the solutions?

Chapter 6.

The new technologies

Document 1

Stressed by e-mails

Millions of messages produce new careers for consultants

A few years ago, e-mail invaded the world, prompting people to race to the keyboard with anticipation, punctuating their sign-offs with smiley faces or TTYL (talk to you later).

But now that it has become an essential form of communication, with traffic exploding from 5.1 million messages in 2000 to 135.6 million messages in 2005, e-mail is causing as much distress as delight. And more and more employers, bosses and workers are trying to find ways to control the load.

Dealing with e-mail – filing it, prioritising it – has added hours of extra work, much of it done by people in the late evening, and early morning.

In a recent survey, 41% of the respondents said they checked their e-mails before going to work. 65% said they would check it on vacation. 4% admitted they had sometimes looked at e-mail in the bathroom!

The situation has given rise to an industry of consultants who advise companies on how to manage e-mail messages, helping executives to improve their job performance.

The Washington Journal, 29 November 2006.

Looking for words

a. courrier électronique : ....

b. pousser à : ....

c. courir : ....

d. clavier : ....

e. signature : ....

f. émoticône : ....

g. plaisir : ....

h. charge : ....

i. traiter : ....

j. trier : ....

k. donner un ordre de priorité : ....

l. étude : ....

m. personne interrogée/sondée : ....

....

n. vérifier : ....

o. toilettes (WC) : ....

p. conseiller : ....

q. gérer : ....

r. cadre : ....

s. améliorer : ....

Figures

a. Complétez les phrases suivantes avec des chiffres trouvés dans le texte.

– .... million e-mails were sent in ....

– .... million messages were sent in ....

– ....% of the respondents say they check their e-mails before going to work, ...% will check their messages on holidays, and ....% admit they look at e-mail in the toilet!

b. Lisez les phrases à haute voix. Que remarquez-vous pour les « . » en anglais ?

c. Qu'ajoute-t-on en anglais entre les centaines et les dizaines ? Que peut-on dire de *million* ?

Document 1 **Practice**

PREMIÈRE PARTIE : REPÉRAGE DE COMPRÉHENSION

1 Exprimez l'idée générale de ce document en français

2 Analysez le titre et le premier paragraphe

Survival kit, p. 167

a. Repérez les mots-clés du titre.
b. Le titre est-il explicite ?
c. Qu'apporte le sous-titre par rapport au titre ?

3 Repérez dans le texte

a. Le nombre de courriers électroniques reçus en 2000 et en 2005.
b. Les problèmes liés à la réception des courriels.
c. Le pourcentage de gens qui consultent leur messagerie le matin avant d'aller travailler.
d. Le pourcentage de ceux qui consultent leurs e-mails en vacances.
e. Le pourcentage de ceux qui admettent le faire dans les toilettes.

4 Vérifiez que vous avez compris

a. Depuis quand communiquons-nous par courrier électronique ?
b. Cette forme de communication était-elle appréciée au début ?
c. Qu'est-ce qui a changé ?
d. Avec quelles conséquences ?
e. Comment réagit-on dans les entreprises ?
f. Que proposent les consultants aux entreprises ?

DEUXIÈME PARTIE : REPÉRAGE DE LANGUE

1 La traduction de « depuis » et de « il y a »

a. Observez la phrase suivante : *E-mail invaded the world a few years ago.*
Quelle est la forme verbale utilisée ? Pourquoi ?

....

b. Observez la phrase suivante : *E-mails have become an essential form of communication since 2005.*
Quelle est la forme verbale utilisée ? Pourquoi ?

....

c. À quoi sert le complément introduit par *since* ?

....

d. Quelle préposition emploie-t-on lorsque l'on veut parler non pas du point de départ, mais du temps écoulé depuis ce point de départ jusqu'au moment présent ?

....

e. Transformez la phrase proposée (1b) en utilisant *for*.

....

f. Complétez les phrases suivantes en utilisant *for*, *since* ou *ago*.

– People started receiving e-mails 5 years ....

– He has been filing his e-mails .... 1 hour.

– She has been checking her messages .... 1 o'clock p.m.!

❷ La construction infinitive

a. Observez la phrase : *Consultants help executives to improve their job performance.*

b. Quel est le sujet de la proposition principale ?

....

c. Quel est le verbe de la proposition principale ?

....

d. Quel est le verbe de la proposition complément ?

....

e. Quel est le sujet de ce verbe ?

....

> **Se construisent de la même manière les verbes qui expriment une volonté, un ordre, une invitation à faire quelque chose, ou le fait de rendre une action possible (= demander à quelqu'un de) : *to allow, to want, to ask, to tell, to expect, to remind, to force, to invite, to persuade, to advise, to recommend, to encourage, to permit, to forbid.***

❸ Traduction en anglais

a. Les employeurs veulent que les salariés soient moins stressés.

....

b. Les consultants encouragent les employeurs à trouver des solutions.

....

c. Les émoticônes rigolos permettent aux gens de sourire.

....

d. Le nombre des courriers électroniques reçus force les employés à gérer leurs messages tard le soir ou tôt le matin.

....

TROISIÈME PARTIE : ACQUISITION DE MÉTHODES

❶ Entraînez-vous au compte rendu oral en anglais

▶ **Survival kit,** p. 171

a. Préparez l'introduction (sources, idée générale du document) en répondant aux questions en *Wh-* en une phrase.

b. Faites un plan du texte
1. Facts
2. Consequences
3. Solutions

c. Préparez la conclusion.

❷ Branching out

▶ **Survival kit,** p. 178

a. Your course includes vocational training and 2 work placements in companies. Could you please report on how the staff communicates in the companies where you worked?

b. Do you receive e-mails? From whom? How do you deal with them?

c. How do you generally communicate? By e-mail? By phone? By SMS? Justify your answer.

Document 2

Danes online with E-revolution

As Jon Larsen's children play on the floor, he is free to work on his laptop computer.

He can check where they are on the waiting list for kindergarten, and he can update his health insurance. Denmark was the first country in the world to make public services available online – and Jon is a big fan. "It's definitely made my life easier," he says. "I used to have big folders full of paperwork, but now I do everything online."

And Denmark is now going a step further, forcing its citizens online. Since the beginning of February for instance, companies dealing with state institutions will have to submit their invoices electronically. Around 15 million transactions that the state previously handled in paper are now managed electronically, with huge benefits. "We have made savings in the public sector of around €100 million (£68.5m)," says a government official, "a big saving in a country of only five million people."

But critics of what is called "e-government" say making this kind of thing compulsory is dangerous. The major concern is for people who don't feel comfortable about new technologies. There is a danger that, as the majority of the population gets used to e-government and e-administration, the small minority who don't know how to use it will get completely marginalized.

The Danish e-invoicing project was given an award for innovation by the European Union, and many other countries are watching the experience closely.

Channel 4 News, July 6, 2006.

---

kindergarten: jardin d'enfants
to update: mettre à jour
available: disponible
folder: dossier
invoice: facture
savings: économies
compulsory: obligatoire

Document 3

Brave New High-Tech World

Not so long ago, texting, also called SMS, was mainly used by young people. The biggest users, in Europe, in the USA and in Asia were the well-off under-30 crowd. And, according to surveys, a majority of young Europeans would choose SMS over actual phone calling, if they were forced to pick one or the other.

Now, texting appears to have joined the letter, phone, fax, and e-mail, as a reliable communications tool for government and companies who are taking advantage of the medium.

Last year, a director sent a 'texto' message to several members of staff over the weekend telling them not to bother coming to work on Monday: they were fired. The boss didn't have to deliver the bad news face to face, and e-mail wouldn't have been appropriate because the employees might not have checked their IN boxes until Monday morning. A message via the cell phone is both instantaneous and private.

Perhaps the best indication that texting has become rooted in our culture is its use by government authorities. Switzerland, where people vote every year, is contemplating a text-voting system nationwide.

But, just as the technology is being accepted, it is changing.

Instant messaging, a faster method of texting, is developing as cell phones and notebooks come with tiny keyboards. Then there's photo and video messaging. Projections suggest that the total messaging market – text, photo, and video – will be worth 50 billion euros, with 2.38 trillion messages sent, by 2010!

The Middleton News, 15 February 2006.

---

well-off: aisé
survey: étude
to pick: choisir
reliable: fiable
to be fired: être viré
to check: vérifier
rooted: enraciné
nationwide: au niveau national
tiny: minuscule
keyboard: clavier

Présentez ces deux textes à l'oral.

Survival kit, p. 171

Document 4

Tele-commuting from a flexi-place

The boom in digital technology has revolutionised the working lives of millions of people. And in the process it has created a growing breed of worker, the tele-worker.

These are the people who use phone and computers to work from home, or from neighbourhood centres, Internet cafes, hotel rooms, clients' premises, on trains and in cars.

Tele-commuters use their laptops with broadband connection and mobile phones to check e-mails and to log on to their companies' systems.

Home-working holds great appeal. There is zero commuting, and also you don't have to spend time with your boss. Add to this a sense of autonomy and you would think home-workers are better off than those who go to the office everyday.

So why aren't more of us working from home?

In fact, many of the home-workers complain of distractions around the house: 40%, for example, say they use part of their time to do household chores (it must be difficult to concentrate when there's washing to do).

Another poll found most home-workers didn't have a dedicated office: 30% use their sitting room, 25% the bedroom and 22% the dining room. And it can be even tougher if you have children.

Balancing work and family, among with the "invasion" of work into the home space, counteracts the benefits of more flexibility and less commuting.

And there are also problems of logistics. Some firms consider it too expensive or inconvenient to have workers at home.

Tele-workers were first counted in 1997. Then, just 981,000 people said they used telephones and computers to work from home or to use their home as a base for work.

They were nearly 2.4 million by early 2005, making up 8% of the working population.

The London News, 10 October 2006.

Looking for words

a. à distance : ....

b. flexible : ....

c. faire la navette entre sa résidence et son lieu de travail : ....

d. travailler à distance : ....

e. télétravailleur (3 mots) : ....

....

f. numérique : ....

g. genre : ....

h. centre d'affaires : ....

i. cyber café : ....

j. locaux : ....

k. ordinateur portable : ....

l. connection rapide (ADSL) : ....

....

m. portable : ....

n. courrier électronique : ....

....

o. se connecter à : ....

p. réseau : ....

q. se plaindre de : ....

r. tâches ménagères : ....

....

s. sondage : ....

t. spécifique : ....

u. difficile : ....

v. harmoniser : ....

w. contrebalancer : ....

x. avantages : ....

y. peu pratique : ....

Document 4 **Practice**

PART 1: UNDERSTANDING THE TEXT

❶ Give the general idea of the article

❷ Analyse the title

▶ Survival kit, p. 167

a. Find the key-words in the title.
b. Try and find how these words were made up.
c. Express the title in your own words.

❸ Find the following information in the article

a. The number of tele-workers in 1997.
b. Their number in 2005.
c. What 8% refers to.
d. The different "flexi-places" tele-workers can perform their duties from.
e. The high-tech equipment tele-workers need to connect to their companies.
f. What rooms home-workers work from when they have no offices at home.

❹ Make sure you have understood the article

a. What is a tele-worker, a tele-commuter?
b. How do tele-workers connect themselves to their companies' systems?
c. List 3 advantages of being a tele-worker.
d. List 3 drawbacks.
e. Why are some companies reluctant to introduce tele-working?

PART 2: ENGLISH LANGUAGE

❶ La réutilisation des mots du texte

a. Complétez le paragraphe avec les mots suivants en rapport avec les nouvelles technologies : *e-mail – digital – broadband – tele-worker – tele-working – connections – Internet – tele-commuter – computer – phone – logging – cyber – laptop – mobile – systems*.

The number of .... (also called ....) has more than doubled since 1997 in the UK. These employees don't work in traditional offices. They work from their homes, ... themselves on to their companies' .... with .... and .... Or their homes are a base, and they work from any place, and check their .... from hotel rooms, ... cafes, and clients' premises. .... is developing thanks to .... technology. .... computers and .... phones have become user-friendly, and .... has made .... on to the .... much faster.

b. Traduisez le texte ci-dessus en français.

❷ Les formes verbales : *preterit* ou *present perfect*

a. Comparez les deux traductions du passé composé français ci-dessous.

– *She has bought a new mobile phone:* elle a acheté un nouveau téléphone portable.

– *She bought a new mobile phone yesterday:* elle a acheté un nouveau téléphone portable hier.

b. Dans quelle phrase le passé composé exprime-t-il une action passée coupée avec le présent ?

....

c. Comment le verbe est-il traduit en anglais ?

....

....

....

d. Dans l'autre phrase, le passé composé exprime un bilan au présent d'une action passée. Comment cette notion est-elle exprimée en anglais ?

....

....

....

e. Complétez à présent les phrases suivantes en vous posant les mêmes questions.

– This morning Jane .... the children to school before sitting at her desk (to take).

– Tele-working .... her to find a balance between private and professional life (to enable).

– She .... the telephone at 10 a.m. to speak to her manager (to use).

– Then she .... for 2 hours on a presentation for the company's Human Resources manager (to work).

– 4 p.m.: the children are back from school. They .... a good day (to have).

❸ La traduction de « le/la... de », avec *the... of*, un génitif ou un mot composé

a. Trouvez l'équivalent dans le texte des groupes nominaux suivants et repérez les constructions employées en anglais.

– L. 3 : la vie de millions de gens : ....

– L. 5 : une nouvelle génération de travailleurs : ....

– L. 11 : les chambres d'hôtel : ....

– L. 12 : les locaux des clients : ....

– L. 18 : les réseaux des entreprises : ....

– L. 24 : un sentiment d'autonomie : ....

b. Traduisez les groupes nominaux suivants avec l'une des trois constructions repérée ci-dessus.

– La vie de centaines d'enfants : ....

– Un sentiment de liberté : ....

– Le portable du directeur : ....

– Des ordinateurs de bureau : ....

❹ Les mots de liaison

Complétez le paragraphe suivant avec les expressions proposées : *as a result – moreover – furthermore – on the one hand – on the other hand – consequently – whereas – nevertheless.*

In the past everybody used to commute to the office every morning, ..., nowadays, there are people who work from home or from flexible places.
....................................., the way people live and work is changing. ...., tele-working makes it possible for workers to live in pleasant surroundings, in villages where houses and flats are much cheaper than in cities.
....................................., it is a way for women to keep a job while their children are young.
....................................., tele-workers often suffer from isolation. ...., they feel excluded from office life, and ...., working from home is often discriminated against as a "woman's job". ...., it is not increasing at the rate people thought it would.

❺ La traduction de « plus » et de « moins » par des formes comparatives

a. Repérez dans le texte des formes comparatives.
- L. 26 : *home-workers are...*
- L. 44 : *it can be even...*
- L. 49 : *it counteracts the benefits of...*

b. Comment exprime-t-on la supériorité ou l'infériorité dans ces trois phrases ?

....

....

....

....

c. Traduisez.
- Les gens travaillent-ils mieux chez eux ?

....

....

....

....

- Ils sont plus autonomes, passent moins de temps en transport et ont plus de temps pour leurs enfants, mais ils travaillent plus d'heures.

....

....

....

....

- Leur travail est plus efficace, plus rentable, grâce aux connections haut débit plus rapides.

....

....

....

6 Les prépositions

Complétez le texte ci-dessous avec les prépositions suivantes : *between* – *to* – *in* – *on* – *by* – *with* – *of* – *from* – *onto*. Certaines prépositions peuvent être utilisées plusieurs fois.

Tele-workers do not work .... companies' offices. They work .... home, or .... trains, and .... cars. They appreciate not having to commute ....the office every day. They log .... their companies' intranets .... computer, and they are autonomous in their everyday working life.

But, they often complain .... isolation and .... not communicating enough .... their colleagues.

Finding a good balance .... private and professional life is not easy.

PART 3: PRACTISING FOR THE EXAM

1 Faites un compte rendu oral du texte

Survival kit, p. 171

a. Préparez l'introduction (sources, idée générale du document) en répondant aux questions en *Wh-* en une phrase.

b. Faites un plan du texte.
1. Facts (Who? How many? How?)
2. Advantages
3. Drawbacks

c. Préparez la conclusion.

2 Rédigez un résumé du texte en français en 110 mots (+/– 10 %) avec des mots de liaison.

Survival kit, p. 173

3 Traduisez le début du texte : de la ligne 1 jusqu'à "systems" (l. 18).

Survival kit, p. 175

4 Branching out

Would you like to work from home? Justify your answer.

Document 5

A new package

Traditional tour firms compete with the Internet packaged holiday.

Minorca or Majorca? It is that time of the year again the brochures are piling up in travel agencies while newspapers and magazines are full of advice about where to go. But the traditional British innovation that provided many people their first experience of warm sand, is no longer what it was. […]

Two things have changed the way Britons research and book their holidays: low-cost airlines and the Internet. Instead of buying a ready-made package consisting of a flight, hotel, car-hire and assorted entertainment from a tour operator's brochure, it is now easy to put together a trip using an online travel agent like Expedia or Travelocity, which last June bought Lastminute.com for £577m ($1billion), or from the proliferating websites of airlines, hotels and car-rental firms.

This has led to restructuring and closures for high-street agents and tour operators, but the traditional firms are starting to fight back, in part by moving more of their business online.

First Choice Holidays, for instance, saw its pre-tax profit rise by 16% to £114m ($196M) last year. Although the overall number of holidays booked has fallen, the company is concentrating on more valuable long-distance and adventure trips. First Choice now sells more than half of its trips directly, via the Internet, over the telephone or from its own travel shops. […]

Some high-street travel agents are also learning to live with the Internet, helping people book complicated trips that they have researched online, providing advice and offering other services.

The Economist, January 7, 2006.
BTS Comptabilité et gestion des entreprises, session juin 2006.

package holiday: voyage tout compris
to pile up: s'empiler
advice: conseils
flight: vol
car-hire/car-rental: location de voiture
high-street: rue commerçante
to fight back: réagir
travel shop: agence de voyages
travel agent: voyagiste

Faites un compte rendu oral de ce texte en anglais.

Survival kit, p. 171

Document 6

The online shopping boom in the UK

Online shopping boomed in the run-up to Christmas 2005, with one in four gifts bought via the Internet.

Consumers spent £4.98 billion online during the ten weeks before December 25, compared with £3.3 billion for the same period a year earlier – a rise of almost 50 per cent. Around 24 million UK consumers shopped online at some point in 2005, spending on average £816 each during the year. The biggest Christmas sellers were toys, computer games, MP3 players, clothing, jewellery, CDs, DVDs, and books.

The figures represent a retail revolution as the nation switches from traditional outlets to the convenience and saving promised by web shopping.

66% of homes in the UK have an Internet connection. Around 8 million have broadband, which allows high-speed Web window shopping and price comparison.

The figures are in tune with reports from Amazon and Tesco, which have both revealed a huge increase in sales in the run-up to Christmas. And FedEx, the US parcel company reported its busiest period ever last December when it handled almost 9 million packages in a single day.

Over the last seven years attitudes towards online shopping have changed considerably. At first people went on the Internet to get good bargains and cheaper goods, but now broadband is so much faster and easier, they find shopping online is just more comfortable and more convenient.

The Internet offers more choice than any other retail marketplace. There are 26,000 shops online. If you lined them up in a row, they would form a high-street 50 miles long, from London to Brighton!

For many companies, the online shopping boom has transformed their business. Toy shop Hamley's, best known for its Regent Street store in London, launched a fully functional online store in 2005. The site attracts 30,000 visitors a week, a fifth of whom make a purchase. On average, customers spend £50 a visit – double the amount they spend in-store.

Company officials predict that in 5 years, the site will become Hamley's most important sales channel.

The Daily News, 21 February 2006.

in tune with: en harmonie avec
bargain: affaire
in a row: l'un derrière l'autre

Looking for words

a. achats en ligne : ……………

b. prospérer : ……………

c. période : ……………

d. précédant : ……………

e. cadeau : ……………

f. jouet : ……………

g. baladeur : ……………

h. bijouterie : ……………

i. chiffre : ……………

j. commerce de détail : ……………

k. passer : ……………

l. magasin (2 mots) : ……………

……………

m. commodité : ……………

n. économie : ……………

o. haut débit : ……………

p. à grande vitesse : ……………

q. lèche-vitrine : ……………

r. paquet (2 mots) : ……………

……………

s. rue commerçante : ……………

t. achat : ……………

u. en moyenne : ……………

v. sur le lieu de vente : ……………

w. vente (2 mots) : ……………

x. circuit : ……………

Document 6 **Practice**

PART 1: UNDERSTANDING THE TEXT

❶ Give the general idea of the article

❷ Analyse the title

Survival kit, p. 167

Answer the following *Wh-* questions: what? Where?

❸ Find the following information in the article

a. What form of trade skyrocketed in the UK in December 2005.
b. The amount spent online by British consumers during the Christmas period.
c. The rise it represents compared to the same period in 2004.
d. What proportion of the British people have got an Internet connection.
e. What "24 million" and "8 million" correspond to.
f. The number of stores online.
g. The distance between London and Brighton (*cf.* map p. 186).
h. The number of visitors on Hamley's website every week.

❹ Make sure you have understood the article

a. How did lots of British people do their Christmas shopping in 2005?
b. What did they buy?
c. What types of companies benefited from the evolution?
d. Why did people shop online before?
e. Why do they use the Internet now?
f. How has Hamley's adapted to the change in people's consuming habits?

PART 2: ENGLISH LANGUAGE

❶ La réutilisation des mots du texte

Complétez le paragraphe suivant en utilisant des mots pris dans le texte.

A lot of British .... did their Christmas .... in 2005. It represents a .... revolution.

People abandon the traditional .... in the ...., and go on .... instead.

.... shopping is very comfortable, easy and .... Connections have become much .... with .... There is more .... online than in .... stores. And you can get good .... when you make a ....

❷ Les comparatifs et les superlatifs

a. Repérez dans le texte 5 adjectifs employés en tant que comparatifs de supériorité.

....

....

....

b. Comment forme-t-on le comparatif d'un adjectif court et d'un adjectif long ?

....

....

c. Repérez dans le texte 3 adjectifs employés en tant que superlatifs.

....

....

d. Comment forme-t-on le superlatif d'un adjectif court et d'un adjectif long ?

....

....

e. Quelle est la différence de sens entre le comparatif et le superlatif ?

....

....

❸ L'emploi des prépositions

Complétez le paragraphe en choisissant parmi les prépositions qui vous sont proposées : *on – from – to – before – by – for – in – with – after – between – during*. Attention, certaines peuvent être utilisées plusieurs fois et d'autres pas du tout.

.... the two months .... Christmas, ... 2005, British shoppers went .... the Internet .... have more choice and .... make bargains. They spent almost £5 billion compared .... the £3.3 billion .... the same period .... 2004.

.... many companies, the new consuming habits adopted .... British shoppers .... their purchases mean they have .... change .... traditional stores, and .... operate both .... high-streets shops and .... the web.

❹ Les formes verbales

a. Repérez dans l'article une phrase au présent simple et justifiez l'emploi de cette forme.

....

....

....

b. Repérez dans l'article une phrase au prétérit et justifiez l'emploi de cette forme.

....

....

....

c. Repérez dans l'article une phrase au *present perfect* et justifiez l'emploi de cette forme.

....

....

....

d. Repérez dans l'article une phrase exprimant une idée de futur et justifiez l'emploi de cette forme.

....

....

....

5 Les mots composés

a. Trouvez dans l'article (l. 42-43) une expression qui désigne un type de magasin et son degré d'opérationnalité.

....

....

....

b. Observez :

– En français, l'ordre des mots est inversé (« un magasin en ligne complètement opérationnel »).
– En anglais, on place le plus près du nom (qui se trouve à la fin) ce qui est le plus important : le secteur, puis le reste.
– Notez qu'en français la phrase est plus longue et comporte souvent des propositions relatives, alors qu'elle est plus compacte en anglais.

c. Construisez des mots composés avec les mots suivants.
- biggest / online / the / sales / Christmas

....

....

....

- fast / connection / Internet / a / broadband

....

....

....

- the / US / parcel / big / company

....

....

....

- 50 / long / a / centre / mile / shopping

....

....

....

6 Les subordonnées avec « si »

a. Observez la phrase suivante du texte (l. 36-38) :

If you lined them up in a row, they would form a high-street 50 miles long, from London to Brighton!

Le verbe, dans la subordonnée commençant par *if*, est au prétérit. Il exprime une condition, une hypothèse irréalisable. Le verbe dans la principale est au conditionnel.

b. Complétez les phrases suivantes (exprimant des hypothèses irréalisables) en employant des formes verbales qui conviennent.
- If everybody (to shop) online, high-street stores (to close).

....

- If high-street stores (to close), city-centres (to become) deserts.

....

- It (to be) fantastic, if everyone in the world (can use) computers.

....

❼ Traduction en anglais

a. Les Britanniques font des achats en ligne car ils trouvent qu'il est plus pratique et plus facile de choisir de chez soi.

....

....

....

b. Les magasins souffriraient s'ils ne s'adaptaient pas à ces nouvelles habitudes de consommation.

....

....

....

c. Il y a quelques années, les consommateurs allaient sur Internet pour obtenir des produits moins chers.

....

....

....

PART 3: PRACTISING FOR THE EXAM

❶ Faites un compte rendu oral en anglais du texte

▶ Survival kit, p. 171

a. Préparez l'introduction.

b. Faites un plan du texte.
1. The online shopping boom
2. Reasons for success
3. How traditional companies react

c. Préparez la conclusion.

❷ Rédigez un compte rendu en français en 160 mots (+/– 10 %)

▶ Survival kit, p. 173

❸ Branching out

a. Compare shopping online and in shopping centres/malls, or in high-streets.

b. What are the dangers of shopping online?

c. Do you shop online? What do you buy?

Document 7

Chinese Revolution turns hi-tech

Sixty years after the revolution engineered by Chairman Mao, China is in the midst of a different revolution – of a digital variety.

Since Mao's death in 1976, China has changed enormously, racing to catch up with the rest of Asia. Mobile phones and cameras have become must-haves – everywhere you go, people are talking, texting, and surfing.

An explosion of capitalism has given cities like Shanghai and Beijing futuristic skylines. Big business and consumer technology alike have found a new home here. The country is already the world's largest producer of mobile phones, PCs and cameras, which it can produce in millions – because of China's biggest resource: people.

On size alone, it is fast becoming a technology superpower and it almost has no choice in the matter. For example, even though only 8% of its people have access to the Internet, this equates to 100 million people online, second only to the US.

No longer just a tech producer, China is becoming a gargantuan tech consumer. It will come as little surprise that China is now the world's largest cell phone market, with more than 380 million mobiles. And, just like internet penetration, the number is rising at an impressive rate. Just like the rest of the world, the Chinese are in love with their phones.

People are surprised by China because it's been like a sleeping lion for years. Now it's starting to jump. China is so ready to compete with US technology that, in one particular case, it bought the company. In December 2004, Chinese PC manufacturer Lenovo did the unthinkable – it bought part of IBM. The part, that is, that makes PCs. Lenovo was already China's largest PC maker but after the IBM deal, it has shot up from 9th largest to 3rd largest PC manufacturer in the world.

China has the size, and it is showing signs of determination to expand its influence beyond its borders.

BBC News Online, 6 January 2006.

BTS Comptabilité et gestion des organisations, session 2006.

digital: numérique
must-have: incontournable
skyline: horizon
rate: rythme
border: frontière

Faites un compte rendu oral de ce texte en anglais.

Survival kit, p. 171

Document 8

Les cartes au trésor de l'Internet

Localiser un cordonnier, trouver un hôtel, calculer son itinéraire, observer sa maison par satellite... Les cartes fleurissent sur le web et les internautes y sont accros. Plus de 13 millions de Français consultent régulièrement les sites Mappy (filiale des Pages Jaunes), Viamichelin et Maporama. Sans oublier le succès phénoménal de geoportail.fr, qui présente des photos-satellite de la France. [...]

Ces services gratuits pour les internautes cachent un véritable business. Une dizaine d'enseignes, comme Avis, Flunch ou France Telecom, rémunèrent mappy.fr pour figurer en bonne place sur ses cartes. En cliquant sur « hôtel », on voit apparaître ceux du groupe Accor, même si ces établissements ne sont pas les plus proches. « C'est d'autant plus efficace que les gens ne perçoivent pas immédiatement ces liens sponsorisés comme une publicité, mais comme un service », confie Fabienne Latzague, directrice de viamichelin.com.

Les géants américains Google, Microsoft et Yahoo se sont lancés dans la bataille. Le premier moteur de recherche mondial vient d'inaugurer Google Maps en France. Pour la première fois, on peut visualiser une adresse sur une carte, une image satellite, ou la combinaison des deux. Il suffit ensuite de taper « pizzeria » ou « pressing » pour afficher les établissements du voisinage. « Le marché va se chiffrer en milliards de dollars », estime Ludovic Broquereau, directeur marketing de Maporama.

Ce n'est pas tout. Google, Mappy et Michelin déclinent aussi leurs services sur les téléphones portables. Une nouvelle opportunité pour les annonceurs. Monoprix ou les salons de coiffure Jacques Dessange envoient déjà des SMS publicitaires aux habitants des grandes villes où ils sont implantés.

Les mobiles font saliver les grandes enseignes. Certaines voudraient localiser (avec leur accord) les utilisateurs de portables, pour leur proposer une réduction dès qu'ils passent à moins de 500 mètres d'une boutique. « Mais les opérateurs s'y opposent », explique Alexandre Mars, PDG de Phonevalley, numéro un français de la publicité sur téléphone. Orange, SFR et Bouygues ne souhaitent pas apparaître comme des Big Brother. Pour combien de temps ? Depuis le mois de mars, la start-up Illico.net propose aux clients d'Orange un service qui permet de localiser leurs enfants via leur mobile.

Le Journal du dimanche, Yann Philippin, 30 juillet 2006.

Questions

1. What can French people currently do thanks to online mapping services and cellphones?

2. How do companies use this new niche?

3. What are the drawbacks of such an evolution?

Chapter 1. Firms

1. Success of companies

1 Firms need to apply the 5 Ps of the marketing mix to sell

a. a good Product which:
- answers a need,
- corresponds to a new trend,
- applies quality imperatives,
- is environmentally-friendly,

b. at the right Price (with the best quality-price ratio),
c. in the right Place,
d. with adequate Promotion,
e. and appropriate Packaging.

2 Firms need to project a positive image of the firm

Nowadays, firms must differentiate themselves from their competitors and show they are good corporate citizens by caring about:

a. the quality of the product manufactured,
b. the quality of their employment and working conditions all over the world:
- in developing countries: fair labour practices,
- in industrialized countries: equal recruitment practices (without considering race, sex, handicap or private life),

c. the major current issues:
- the unemployed, the homeless, sick people, racism, obesity, etc.,
- life in our society: community actions, environment problems, sports sponsoring, etc.

3 Firms need to have efficient management

a. Good managers know their business:
- they are experts with know-how in a specific field,
- they are creative, innovative, and always look for new niches.

b. Good managers know their staff:
- they know how to use all the resources in the firm, particularly human resources,
- they motivate their staff with incentives, quality circles, perks or promotion.

CAN YOU ANSWER?
1. What are the 5 Ps of the marketing mix?
2. What is a corporate citizen company?
3. What is a "good" manager?

Words, words, words...

1

environmentally-friendly: écologique
firm (company, business, corporation): entreprise, société
marketing mix: plan de marchéage
need: besoin
quality imperatives: objectifs de qualité
ratio: rapport
trend (tendency): tendance

2

competitor: concurrent
corporate citizen: entreprise citoyenne
current issues: problèmes d'actualité
developing countries: pays en voie de développement
equal recruitment practices: égalité des chances à l'embauche
fair labour practices: conditions de travail justes/humaines/correctes

3

field: domaine
incentive: stimulation
know-how: savoir-faire
management: personnel d'encadrement
niche: créneau
perk: avantage en nature
staff: personnel

2. The organization of companies

1 Types of companies

The most common are:

a. Private limited/limited liability companies (Ltd)
Their shares are not quoted on the Stock Exchange.

b. Public limited companies (PLC or plc)
Their shares are quoted and traded on the Stock Exchange.

c. A company is organized into different departments
– It has a head office/headquarters.
– It can also have subsidiaries which report to the parent company.

2 The organization chart

a. The organization differs according to the size of the company:
giant multinational/global structure, corporation, small- or medium-sized firm.

b. The chain of command

Top Management ▶ Middle Management ▶ Supervisory Management ▶ Operatives

1. Chairman (US: president)
S/he heads the Board of Directors and supervises the activities of the company.

2. Managing Director (MD) or Chief Executive Officer (CEO)
S/he manages the company.

3. Officers reporting directly to the MD (functional positions)
– Company Secretary
– General Office Manager (can take care of Personnel/Human Resources, Risk Management, Legal Matters, Audit and control)

4. Departments (operational positions)

4a. Production Director
▶ R&D
▶ Purchasing
▶ Manufacturing
▶ Warehouse
▶ Transport

4b. Sales and Marketing Director
▶ Sales
▶ Marketing
▶ Advertising

4c. Finance Director
▶ Accounts
▶ IT (Computing)

4d. Human Resources
▶ Recruitment
▶ Training
▶ Employee relations

CAN YOU ANSWER?
1. What is a PLC?
2. What are Human Resources staff in charge of?

Words, words, words...

1

department: service
parent company: société mère
private limited company (Ltd): société à responsabilité limitée (SARL)
public limited company (plc): société anonyme (SA)
quoted: coté
share: action
Stock Exchange: Bourse
subsidiary: filiale

2

accounts department: service comptabilité
chairman: président
chief executive officer (CEO): directeur général
IT (information technology): informatique
managing director (MD): directeur général
organization chart: organigramme
purchasing department: service des achats
sales department: service commercial
small- or medium-sized firm: petite ou moyenne entreprise
training: formation
warehouse: entrepôt

3. Problems of companies

1 Internal problems

They are related to the firm itself. They can be due to:

a. Inefficient production
The tools or assembly lines can be old-fashioned.

b. The marketing strategy
It is not adapted.

c. The management
It is inefficient. Managers and senior executives can be too old, or not dynamic enough.

d. Social problems
Strikes or other disputes may slow down or stop production.

e. Financial problems
- The overheads are too high (manufacturing/labour/running/financial costs).
- The firm makes no profits and is in the red.
- The shareholders no longer trust it.
- The firm is overstaffed and needs restructuring.

f. Problems of image
Accidents may endanger a firm's reputation.

2 External problems

These problems are related to the business environment. They can be due to:

a. Suppliers
- The cost of raw materials may increase.
- Delivery becomes difficult.
- Suppliers decide to leave the firm.
- Banks refuse to finance the firm any longer.

b. Sales
- Saturation of the market.
- Changes in buying patterns at home, or different patterns abroad.

c. Competition
- At home, or abroad (other companies, currency devaluations or cheap labour costs).

d. Regulations
- New laws, deregulation and globalization have made the market more competitive.
- Taxes, tariffs, quality labels, ecolabels and standards may limit exports.

CAN YOU ANSWER?

1. Describe the internal problems companies may have to face.
2. What problems are linked to the business environment?

Words, words, words...

1

assembly line: chaîne de montage
to be in the red: faire des pertes, être dans le rouge
manufacturing/labour/running/financial costs: coûts de production/salariaux/de fonctionnement/financiers
overheads: frais généraux
overstaffed: en sureffectif
shareholder: actionnaire
strike: grève
tool: outil

2

abroad: à l'étranger
competition: concurrence
currency: devise
delivery: livraison
deregulation: déréglementation
ecolabel: label vert
globalization: mondialisation
patterns: comportements
quality label: label de qualité
raw material: matière première
regulation: réglementation
standard: norme
supplier: fournisseur
tariff: barrière douanière
tax: impôt

4. Solutions for companies

To be profitable or survive, firms can, for example:

1 Reduce costs

a. Streamline operations globally and internally.
b. Close unprofitable operations, and sell non-vital assets.
c. Cut jobs, or introduce flexible working hours.
d. Subcontract some of their production, or outsource services (cleaning, catering, transport).
e. Relocate or outsource production abroad to profit from lower labour costs in developing countries or avoid export problems (quotas, currency problems, regulations).
f. Limit expenses.

2 Adapt

a. Restore the partners' confidence (customers, suppliers, bankers, investors).
b. Retrain the staff.
c. Review their purchasing policy.
d. Invest in innovation with Research and Development.
e. Look for new niches and launch new products to adapt to new needs, or diversify production, invest in automation.
f. Modernize their activities and adopt just-in-time strategies to reduce inventories.
g. Improve the distribution network (franchising, for example).
h. Adapt to the local demand.
i. Adopt corporate citizen attitudes.
j. Advertise to inform the public about new products.
k. Tap profitable new markets.
l. Merge with another firm.
m. Make partnership and joint-venture deals.
n. Look for new financial resources (from shareholders...).
o. Focus on their core activities.

CAN YOU ANSWER?

1. How can a firm restore investors' confidence?
2. Why do some companies relocate their production and services abroad?
3. How can a company increase its profits?

Words, words, words...

1

assets: actif
to avoid: éviter
catering: restauration
currency: devise
globally: mondialement
job: emploi
to outsource : externaliser
to relocate: délocaliser
to streamline: dégraisser, restructurer
to subcontract: sous-traiter
unprofitable: non rentable

2

to advertise: faire de la publicité
core: central
corporate citizen: entreprise citoyenne
customer: client
distribution network: réseau de distribution
inventory: stock
just-in-time: juste-à-temps
to launch: lancer
to merge: fusionner
niche: créneau
partnership: partenariat
purchasing policy: politique des achats
supplier: fournisseur
to tap (markets): attaquer
to train: former

Activities

❶ Vocabulaire

Complétez le texte à l'aide des mots proposés. Chaque mot ne peut servir qu'une fois, certains mots ne seront pas utilisés.

Liste de mots : *ambitious - community - company - experience - experiment - failure - field - know-how - manager - payroll - risks - staff - success.*

A good .... knows how to motivate her/his ....,

s/he is an expert in his/her ....: s/he has ....

S/he is .... for her/his firm. S/he is ready to take

.... and sees .... as an improving

.... S/he is also active in her/his ....

❷ Traduction

Traduisez les phrases ci-dessous en anglais.

– Une entreprise réussit si elle vend un bon produit, au bon endroit, au juste prix, avec une promotion appropriée.

....

....

– De nos jours, beaucoup d'entreprises soutiennent de grandes causes humanitaires. Parfois, elles s'engagent aussi localement.

....

....

– Les entreprises citoyennes s'intéressent à la qualité du produit fabriqué.

....

....

– Cette entreprise vend des produits avec un bon rapport qualité-prix, mais ses coûts de fonctionnement sont trop élevés.

....

....

– Nous allons délocaliser au Royaume-Uni pour profiter des coûts salariaux moins élevés.

....

....

– Ils sont dans le rouge et seront obligés de réduire leurs coûts avec des licenciements.

....

....

– Ils veulent également s'attaquer aux marchés émergents, là où se trouvent de nombreux clients potentiels.

....

....

❸ Travail de compréhension sur les titres ▶ Survival kit, p. 167

a. Lisez les titres suivants.

1. FRANCE TURNS ORANGE

2. Changes at Body Shop Lift 6-Month Profit

3. Body Shop Gains on Takeover Talk

4. Marks & Spencer to Quit Continent

5. Philips Pulls Plug

6. U.K. Bank To Eliminate 6,000 Jobs To Cut Costs

7. Siemens to Shed 3,500 More Jobs

b. Identifiez, par un repérage couleur, les mots-clés des titres.

c. Les titres 4 à 7 ne sont pas des énoncés complets sur le plan grammatical. Réécrivez-les en ajoutant les éléments syntaxiques qui manquent.

....

....

....

....

....

d. Lisez les huit articles. Indiquez pour chacun le numéro du titre correspondant.

A. Once one of Britain's business success stories, the retailer Marks & Spencer PLC on Thursday announced its most radical ever restructuring, with plans to sell its U.S. units and to withdraw from Continental Europe.

Titre n° ☐

B. Siemens AG, Germany's biggest engineering company, said Thursday it was cutting a further 3,500 jobs after second-quarter profit fell 11 percent, hurt by lower demand for mobile phones and semiconductors.

Titre n° ☐

C.

Standard Chartered PLC, a British-based bank with most of its operations in Asia, said Wednesday it would carve 6,000 jobs out of its 35,000 global work force in $715 million effort to lower costs.

Titre n° ☐

D.

France Telecom SA said it would bring all of its French mobile-phone operations under the Orange brand name.

Titre n° ☐

E.

Body Shop International PLC said Thursday that its first-half profit rose 12 percent in the six months through Aug. 26 after it introduced new products, refurbished stores and cut costs in its U.S. operations.

Titre n° ☐

F.

Swissair Group, seeking to get back on a sound financial course, said Tuesday that it planned to eliminate jobs and shift around managers as part of a restructuring aimed at saving about 500 million Swiss francs ($279 million) in the second half of the year.

Titre n° ☐

G.

The Body Shop, once an icon of alternative business practices and the use of natural products for its beauty lotions and shampoos, acknowledged Thursday that it was in talks to sell its 1,840 stores to Grupo Omnilife, an upstart Mexican company with a rags-to-riches story similar to its own.

Titre n° ☐

H.

Philips Electronics NV said Tuesday that it would stop making mobile phones and hand over control of a China-based joint venture to its partner, China Electronics Corp., as it becomes the latest cell-phone maker to exit the business.

Titre n° ☐

e. Identifiez dans chaque article, par un repérage couleur, les mots-clés qui correspondent aux mots-clés de son titre.

f. Trouvez un titre pour l'article qui n'en a pas.

....

g. Préparez une phrase d'introduction à propos des entreprises Philips et Body Shop.

....

....

....

....

❹ Questions en anglais

a. Does McDonald's apply the 5 Ps of the marketing mix? Justify your answer about the 5 different Ps.

....

....

....

b. Give examples of French companies who show they care for the environment.

....

....

c. Give examples of sports events which are sponsored by companies.

....

....

d. Give examples of unfair labour practices.

....

....

e. What is the difference between Ltd and plc companies?

....

....

....

❺ Analyse de graphiques

Survival kit, p. 185

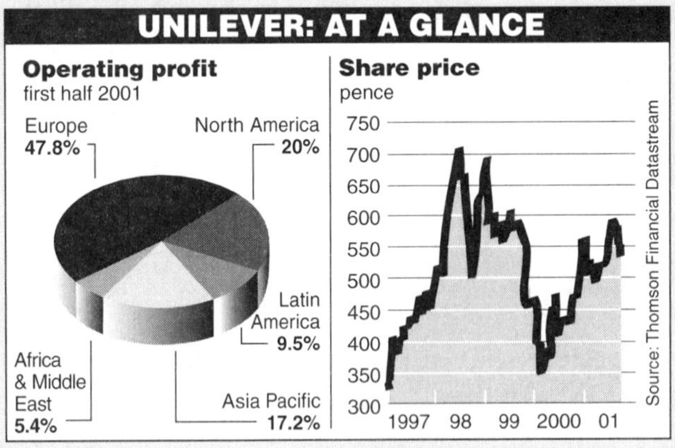

Unilever is an Anglo-Dutch consumer-product multinational company.

The Independent, 25 September 2001.

a. Comment upon the geographical distribution of Unilever's profits.

....

....

....

b. Study the evolution of the share price between 1997 and 2001.

....

....

....

Chapter 2. Work

1. Unemployment: facts and trends

1 A major issue since 1980

– In the early 1980s, every industrialized country (apart from Japan) was affected by high unemployment rates (over 10%).
– In the mid and the late 1980s, unemployment plummeted in the UK and in the USA whereas it remained high in continental Europe.
– In the late 1990s, the joblessness rate fell everywhere with the emergence of new forms of work.
– Since 2000, unemployment rates have been fluctuating with the evolution of basic economic factors (production, consumption and distribution).
– They were also influenced by political and economic events taking place in other countries.

2 The role of governments

To create jobs, governments can adopt various solutions:

a. Tax
– Protect domestic firms with taxes on foreign imports.
– Help firms reduce their costs with lower corporate taxes and/or interest rates.
– Reduce certain consumption taxes.

b. Training
– Improve initial schooling, lifetime training and retraining programmes.
– Encourage young people to study longer: this reduces the number of new workers.
– Adapt training to the needs of companies.

c. Legislation
– Less red tape and fewer legal restrictions for young firms.
– Encourage early retirement measures.
– Reduce the workweek.
– Ban overtime.
– Pass laws that make it more difficult for companies to make people redundant, and impose retraining.

d. Money
– Help firms to hire people with subsidies.
– Reform benefits: either reduce them to cut costs, or increase them to boost household consumption.

CAN YOU ANSWER?

1. Compare the importance of unemployment in the early 1980s and nowadays.
2. How can governments encourage the creation of jobs?

Words, words, words...

1

issue: problème
the early ...: au début
the late ...: à la fin
the mid ...: au milieu
to plummet: dégringoler
unemployment/joblessness: chômage

2

benefits: avantages sociaux
to boost: dynamiser
corporate tax: impôt sur les sociétés
domestic: national
early retirement: retraite anticipée
to hire: embaucher
household consumption: consommation des ménages
legislation: lois
to make people redundant: mettre des personnes au chômage
overtime: heures supplémentaires
red tape: formalités administratives
subsidies: subventions
tax: impôt
training: formation

2. Reasons accounting for unemployment

1 Globalization of business and fierce global competition for market share

a Competition from cheap labour-cost countries
Multinational companies now think global: they relocate production to reduce their costs, become more competitive and increase their profits.

b. Development of IT and automation
Investments in new technologies, especially information and automation, make it possible to produce at low costs in far-away countries.

c. Mergers and acquisitions: companies restructure, making employees redundant.

d. Return On Equities demanded by shareholders
If profitability is unsatisfactory, PLCs streamline their operations, close unprofitable plants and lay off staff to increase efficiency.

2 High labour costs due to benefits and perks

a. Welfare policies
After World War II, governments implemented expensive welfare policies which guaranteed workers many advantages/benefits from cradle to grave.
- Paid holidays.
- Free health care.
- Family help: maternity leave, subsidized day nurseries, holiday camps, student grants, school lunches.
- Subsidized housing and transport.
- Pension schemes, early-retirement schemes.
- Unemployment benefits, retraining schemes.

b. Perks
Companies also offered their staff: bonuses on special occasions, company car and company shares, discounts on company products, cheap loans and mortgages, extra holidays.

3 The baby-boom generation

The many people who were born after World War II have not retired yet.

4 The rising importance of stock markets

Companies need funds to invest. They will get them only if investors have confidence in the company and choose to invest thanks to a satisfactory return on equity.

CAN YOU ANSWER?
1. Where are employees well protected?
2. Why are labour costs lower in market-oriented countries?

Words, words, words...

1

automation: robotisation
merger: fusion
profit: bénéfice
Return On Equities: retour sur fonds propres
shareholder: actionnaire

2

bonus: prime
day nursery: crèche
early retirement: retraite anticipée
free health care: Sécurité sociale gratuite
from cradle to grave: du berceau à la tombe
grant: bourse (d'étude)
labour cost: coût de main-d'œuvre
to lay off: licencier
loan: prêt
market-oriented policies: libéralisme
minimum wage: salaire minimum
mortgage: prêt hypothécaire
paid holidays: congés payés
pension scheme: plan de retraite
perks: avantages en nature
retraining scheme: recyclage, formation
share: action
subsidized housing: allocation logement
subsidized transport: transport financé pour partie par l'employeur
unemployment benefit: allocation chômage
welfare policies: interventionnisme

3

to retire: prendre sa retraite

4

to invest: investir

3. New trends in working life

1 Flexibility

a. Definition

Workers no longer have full-time, life-long permanent jobs.

Companies adopt new work schedules, just-in-time, flexible working hours, job-sharing, temping or temporary jobs on fixed-term contracts (workers carry out specific tasks in a company, then leave), on a part-time or full-time basis.

b. Consequences

– Salaries are annualized, or people get paid by the hour, or for a mission.
– Employees accept odd jobs and work when companies need them, part-time, full-time, or overtime according to the demand.
– Working at the weekends, and/or at night, in shifts has become normal.

c. Advantages for the companies

– They save on labour costs.
– Just-in-time production (round the clock, i.e. 24 hours a day, 7 days a week) enables them to respond to demand quickly, to increase productivity and to reduce costly inventories.
– Savings are made on transport, tax and customs duties if production is kept at home.

d. Advantages for the workers

– Jobs are created, or kept, and not relocated abroad: a number of the unemployed can re-enter the working community.
– Employees can work and have more free-time (for leisure, studies, family, children).

e. Drawbacks for the workers

– Their private lives come after the company's demands!
– They have the same stress as before, without having the same advantages (no job security, few benefits and perks).
– Psychological drawbacks: a real job is thought of as a full-time, life-long job. Temping, all the more so if it is part-time, is often regarded as women's work.

2 Telecommuting, teleworking and teleservice jobs

a. Definition

Telecommuting means:
– working from any place except the office (home, car, etc.),
– keeping in touch with the company thanks to the development of modern communication techniques (phone, fax, PC networks, Intranets, the Internet, etc.).

b. Why telecommuting has developed

– Lower real-estate expenses.
– Reducing the cost of equipment and office overheads.
– Less pollution (fewer workers use their car).
– Gains of time and of productivity (staff working from home tend to take less sick leave).
– More flexibility and autonomy for the staff.
– More profitability when workers can't go to the office (natural disasters, explosions, strikes or terrorist attacks).

c. Evolution

Companies tend to use virtual offices: they give up traditional office-buildings, and offer their nomadic staff hot-desking facilities only.
– Fewer work-stations than members of staff.
– Employees rent work-stations equipped with phone lines and PCs for a few hours from time to time: her/his files are brought in only when s/he comes.

d. Restrictions

– Employees worry about their career prospects and promotion opportunities.
– Absence of teamwork and communication.
– Isolation of employees, distraction from neighbours, lack of self-discipline, feeling that home is no longer a refuge from the office.

3 Entrepreneuring

a. Definition

Many small companies, or start-ups, have appeared on the market.

They can be: microentreprises employing fewer than 10 people, small- or medium-sized firms, subcontractors for large companies.

They are specialized in services: helping people in their everyday life, or specialized in digital media (designing Web pages, programming links, looking for information on the Internet or producing images).

b. Problems

Fragile companies: they rely on a booming economy.

In Europe, they find it hard to raise capital to invest, compared with the USA.

4 Teamwork

Companies stress the importance of employee involvement and feeling of responsibility. The staff should share goals, improve products and processes, reduce human error, try harder for the company to be competitive and successful.

Employers motivate the workforce with performance-related pay, employee ownership, profit-sharing and stock-option schemes.

5 An aging population

- The baby-boomers, born after World War 2, will retire in the next 20 years.
- Young people have fewer babies than in the past.
- People realize their incomes will considerably decrease when they become pensioners.
- Companies fear shortages of skilled staff, and governments are facing problems to finance pensions, healthcare, and public services.
- The current trend is towards working longer to get additional income.

CAN YOU ANSWER?

1. What forms of employment are developing nowadays?
2. Do the workers benefit or lose in the process?
3. What types of micro-company can create jobs?

Words, words, words...

1

fixed-term contract: CDD (contrat à durée déterminée)
full-time: à temps plein
inventory: stock
job-sharing: partage d'un emploi
just-in-time: flux tendu, juste-à-temps
labour costs: coûts de main-d'œuvre
odd job: petit boulot
overtime: heures supplémentaires
part-time: à temps partiel
permanent job : CDI (contrat à durée indéterminée)
productivity: productivité
to relocate: délocaliser
schedule: planning
shift: équipe
staff: personnel
task: tâche
temping: emploi précaire, intérim
working hours: horaires (de travail)

2

career prospects: perspectives de carrière
expense: dépense, frais
file: dossier
hot-desking facilities: possibilité d'accès à un bureau virtuel
network: réseau
office: bureau
overheads: frais généraux
profitable: rentable
real estate: immobilier
to rent: louer
sick leave: congé maladie
strike: grève
teamwork: travail d'équipe
telecommuting: télétravail, travail à distance
work-station: poste de travail

3

small- or medium-sized firm: petite ou moyenne entreprise

4

involvement: investissement personnel
performance-related pay: salaire en fonction des résultats
profit-sharing: intéressement
stock-option schemes: plans d'intéressement en actions
workforce : personnel

5

healthcare: dépenses de santé
income: revenu
pension/er: retraite/retraité
to retire: prendre sa retraite
shortage: pénurie

Activities

❶ Vocabulaire

Complétez le texte à l'aide des mots proposés. Chaque mot ne peut servir qu'une fois, certains mots ne seront pas utilisés.

Liste de mots : *temps - dismiss - early retirement - employed - paid holidays - income - working hours - perk - job - jobless - pensioners - labour force - unemployment - fixed-term - boomers - retire - lay-offs - benefits - permanent - full-time - to work.*

The .... rate is higher in continental Europe than in GB and the USA, because .... is too expensive. Europeans generally take longer .... and .... earlier than the rest of the world. .... are very costly for companies who therefore hesitate to hire .... employees for .... jobs and resort to .... and .... contracts.

Several countries have tried to reduce unemployment by encouraging .... before 60, or by reducing .... Nowadays, baby .... are encouraged to .... longer to get additional .... when they become ....

❷ Traduction

Traduisez les phrases ci-dessous en anglais.

– Beaucoup d'entreprises délocalisent la production dans des pays où la main-d'œuvre est bon marché.

....

– Ainsi, elles peuvent réduire leurs coûts et accroître leurs bénéfices.

....

– De plus en plus de gens font actuellement de l'intérim et sont embauchés avec des CDD.

....

– Grâce au télétravail, les entreprises peuvent réduire leurs coûts immobiliers et les coûts de fonctionnement.

....

....

– Avec les horaires de travail flexibles, les employés travaillent quand l'entreprise a besoin d'eux.

....

– Ils sont payés à l'année et travaillent à temps partiel, à temps complet ou en heures supplémentaires, selon la demande.

....

....

– Le flux tendu permet de réduire les stocks qui coûtent cher.

....

❸ Travail de compréhension sur les titres

Survival kit, p. 167

Pour chaque article :
a. Lisez le titre.
b. Identifiez, par un repérage couleur, les mots-clés qui répondent aux questions en *Wh-*.
c. Lisez le paragraphe qui suit.
d. Indiquez sous chaque article les informations qu'apporte le premier paragraphe par rapport au titre.

1. **Home computers tie workers to the office**

Far from helping people balance their office and home lives, portable computers and mobile phones make employees feel they have to be available for work around the clock.

Metro, August 6, 2001.

....

....

....

2. **Japan's jobless total is worst on record**

Unemployment in Japan soared in July to its worst level since records began in 1953, the Government confirmed. In the year to July, the number of unemployed rose 230,000 to 3.3m – 5pc of the workforce.

The Weekly Telegraph, September 2001.

....

....

....

3. **Wages are £2,000 higher in the South**

Earnings in London and the South-East are outstripping the rest of the country by more than 20 per cent, adding to fears of a deepening North-South divide.

Metro, July 23, 2001.

....

....

....

4. **UK jobs to go as Gap cuts 800 after fall in sales**

The US's leading fashion chain, The Gap, is planning to axe nearly 800 more jobs in addition to the 1,300 head office posts it eliminated only last month. Some of the new cutbacks will be in London.

The Guardian, August 10, 2001.

....

....

....

5. **Unemployment at 25-year low**

The number of people out of work has fallen to its lowest level for 25 years, it was announced yesterday. Unemployment fell by 12,000 last month to 963,700, a rate of 3.2 per cent, the best figures since 1975.

Metro, August 6, 2001.

....

....

....

6. **Fujitsu wields axe on 16,400**

JAPANESE computer chip and PC maker Fujitsu is to cut 16,400 jobs worldwide in a restructuring plan which threatens hundreds of UK staff.

Metro, August 21, 2001.

....

....

....

7.

Senior men are more likely to work from home

Researchers from the Institute of Employment Studies (IES) have found that the more senior someone is, the more likely they are to opt for "tele-working", where they are linked to work through a PC and spend at least one day a week working away from the office.

The Independent, January 2000.

....

....

....

....

8.

INEQUALITY STREET

Women are still being paid less for doing the same job as men, according to a new survey. Why is Britain the most sexist country in Europe, asks Cristina Odone.

The Guardian, February 27, 2001.

....

....

....

....

9.

UN Warns of Alarming Rise in Depression at Work

– Stress, anxiety and depression on the job affect as many as one in 10 workers worldwide, and cost employers in Europe and the United States more than $120 billion a year, a study by the United Nations shows.

The Independent, January 2001.

....

....

....

....

10.

French Jobless Rate Rises For First Time in 3 Years

PARIS – France's jobless rate unexpectedly climbed in June for the first time in almost three years, the government said Tuesday, as slowing economic growth prompted companies to freeze hiring.

International Herald Tribune, August 1, 2001.

....

....

....

....

11.

Shift work "unhealthy for employees"

The 24-hour society, which has forced people to work long and irregular hours, is putting the country's health at risk, a study has found.

Metro, August 2001.

....

....

....

12.

Debenhams to create 4,000 jobs at new stores

Debenhams, the department store chain, plans to create 4,000 jobs over the next four years as it opens 11 new stores. The store openings were first announced at the company's half-year results in April but the company only set out the employment details yesterday.

The Independent, September 2000.

....

....

....

....

2

❹ Analyse d'un graphique et d'un article de presse

▶ Survival kit, p. 185

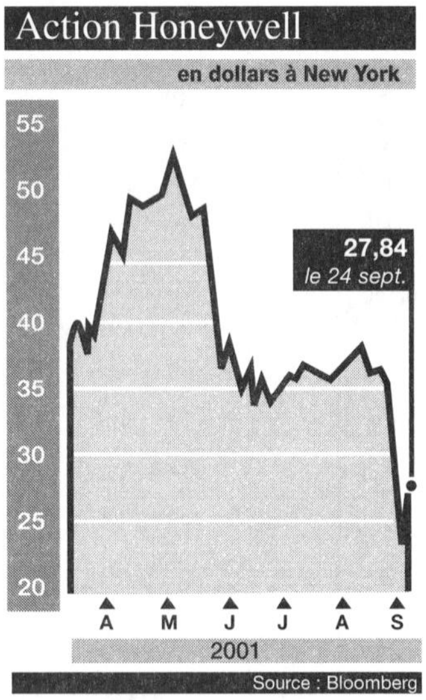

Honeywell supprime 16 000 emplois

HONEYWELL est touché de plein fouet par les difficultés que traversent les compagnies aériennes américaines. Le conglomérat, présent aussi bien dans les équipements aéronautiques, les systèmes de contrôle ou l'énergie, a revu à la hausse, lundi 24 septembre, le nombre de suppressions d'emplois envisagées cette année. Une réduction d'effectifs touchant 4 000 personnes vient s'ajouter aux 12 000 déjà programmées. Au total, l'entreprise devrait se séparer de près de 13 % de ses employés en 2001, et fermer 51 établissements.

Le Monde, 26 septembre 2001.

a. What are the main ideas expressed in the graph and in the article?

....

....

....

b. Study the evolution of the Honeywell share price on the NYSE from April to September 2001.

....

....

....

....

....

....

c. What are the reasons for the problems of Honeywell?

....

....

....

....

....

d. How has the company decided to react?

....

....

....

Chapter 3. Consumers

1. Changes in consuming patterns

1 From the late '60s to the late '80s

a. Our society changed
- Baby boomers became adults, got married, had children, had a career.
- Women worked more and more.
- People went to live in the suburbs and commuted to work every day.
- People went shopping once a week with the family car.

b. What people bought
- A car, a home and household goods to equip it: white goods (washing-machines, dishwashers, etc.) and brown goods (hi-fi equipment, TV sets, videos, etc.).
- FMCGs (fast-moving consumer goods: food, toiletries, cleaning products).
- Brands and disposables (products you throw away after using them).

c. Retailing adapted
Supermarkets and hypermarkets appeared in the '60s.

2 Consumption has changed nowadays due to several factors

a. Changing working patterns (See chapter 2 – Work, p. 125)

b. The globalization of business
- The products we buy are standardized to make economies of scale.
- Agriculture and fishing have been industrialized.

c. The population in industrialized countries is getting older
- Households are saturated with basic products and equipment.
- People worry about their retirement as regards pensions and services.

d. Development of communications
- Computers, mobile phones and the Internet are entering our lives.
- People travel more often, commute to work and go shopping by car.

3 Consequences

a. People buy differently
- They ask for a discount each time they make a purchase: this accounts for the success of sales periods.
- They try to save money and think twice before they buy.
- They want stores to be open late at night and at the weekends.

b. The new mature consumers
- They demand the best quality-price ratio.
- They can boycott products when companies don't behave as corporate citizens.

CAN YOU ANSWER?

1. Compare the consumers of the '70s and the consumers of the '90s.
2. Do you identify with the description of the modern consumer? Give examples.

Words, words, words...

1

brand : marque
to commute: voyager de son domicile à son lieu de travail
FMCGs (fast-moving consumer goods): produits de grande consommation
household: foyer
suburbs: banlieue

2

economie of scale: économie d'échelle
globalization : mondialisation
pension: retraite (indemnité)
retirement: retraite (état)

3

to demand: exiger
quality-price ratio: rapport qualité-prix
sales: périodes de soldes
to save : économiser

2. Current consumer trends

1 Where consumers shop

a. Shopping malls/centres.
b. Hypermarkets and supermarkets for FMCGs.
c. Hard-discounters.
d. DIY stores and garden centres for their leisure activities.
e. Virtual stores on the Internet.
f. Vending machines.
g. Factory outlets/designer discount malls.
h. Mail order companies.

2 New products

a. Convenience food
Convenience foods are frozen or pre-cooked products, takeaway pizzas, UHT milk, etc. They cater to time-pressed people: as women have become part of the workforce and are no longer mere housewives.

b. Organic products
The new fad for these products corresponds to more environmental awareness than before. More and more people are now ready to pay more for products which respect the environment and do not contain pesticides.

3 New strategies

a. Customer loyalty
Companies encourage customers to come back, practising one-to-one marketing. They deliver loyalty cards and use the information they collect on databases to develop customer loyalty.

b. New services
Mail-ordering, home shopping through the Internet, the Minitel or telephone and home delivery help time-pressed consumers.

c. Value-marketing
Firms must show that they are good corporate citizens, concerned with their environment and social issues in their communities: they offer products that have a message.

CAN YOU ANSWER?

1. What type of products are consumers interested in? Why?
2. How do companies attract consumers?
3. How do companies show they are good corporate citizens?

Words, words, words...

1

DIY (do-it-yourself) store: magasin de bricolage
factory outlet/designer discount mall : magasin-entrepôt
hard-discounter : magasin mini-marge
mail order : VPC (vente par correspondance)
to shop: faire des courses
shopping mall/centre: centre commercial
vending machine: distributeur automatique

2

awareness : prise de conscience
to cater to : répondre aux besoins de
convenience food: plats tout préparés
fad : toquade
housewife : femme au foyer
organic products: produits biologiques

3

customer loyalty: fidélité du consommateur
database : base de données
home delivery: livraison à domicile
home shopping: achats à domicile
issue: problème
loyalty card: carte de fidélité

3. The new targets

1 Children (under 11), tweens (from 11 to 13) and teenagers

a. Products
Toys (and video games), food (cereals, biscuits, chocolate bars) and fast food, clothes and sports equipment, health (+ the baby market with nappies, food, milk, etc.).

b. Reasons
- Because of divorces, paradoxically, children have more relatives and get more presents.
- Women work more and buy more to compensate for their absence.
- Social imperatives: teenagers wear famous brands and children ask for branded toys.

c. How business adapts and targets them
- Kids are strong purchase-influencers.
- Companies buy advertising TV-time in children's programmes.

2 Single people

a. Definition
They are divorcees, single parents, single young people and widow(er)s.

b. How they live
Most enjoy their freedom, are affluent and work full-time. They symbolize the fragmentation of our society, a radical change in family values and traditions.

c. How business adapts and targets them
Singles have more free time: they can go out more.
Specific products and services have developed: ready-cooked meals in single portions, smaller appliances, more books and magazines, the cinema.

3 Old people

This section of the population is increasing: one fifth of the children born today will live to be 100 years old.

a. An active segment
Senior citizens drive, travel, shop, etc.
They spend their money on themselves (food, healthcare, homes and entertainment) and their families (presents).

b. How business adapts and targets them
- New products are launched, often easier to use.
- Adapting the salesforce: some shops have recruited older staff to serve their older customers better.
- Adapting their services in aftersales, home deliveries, etc.
- Adapting their advertising campaigns: old people have appeared in commercials (Lacroix, McDonald's, Nivea cosmetics).

CAN YOU ANSWER?
1. What type of consumers are specifically targeted nowadays?
2. Why are old people a very good niche for companies?

Words, words, words...

1
advertising: publicité
nappies (US: diapers): couches-culottes
profitable: rentable
purchase influencer: prescripteur d'achat
relatives: famille

2
divorcee: divorcée
single: célibataire
widow(er): veuve(f)

3
aftersales: après-vente
commercial: spot publicitaire (radio ou télévision)
customer: client
entertainment: loisir
healthcare: services médicaux
home delivery: livraison à domicile
salesforce: force de vente
senior citizen: personne âgée

4. The evolution of payment

1 The different means of payment

The most common are: cash, cheques, cards, bank transfers, drafts and bills of exchange.

2 The different types of cards

They tend to develop very fast.

a. Store cards
They are issued by department stores or hypermarkets. Customers have special discounts or advantages at the checkout (no queues).

b. ATM cards
They are issued by banks so that customers can get cash from ATMs.

c. Debit and credit cards
Debit cards provide no credit facilities: money is withdrawn from your account after each purchase. Credit cards offer credit: money debited at the end of the month.

d. Smart cards
They are called smart cards because the chip in the card can record transactions. It carries the user's PIN number, making the card safer.

e. Cash-cards
They can also be called electronic wallets. In France, pre-paid cards are used to phone or park cars.
Customers download money from their bank accounts onto their cards. Then, they can use the cards for their purchases. Today, new cards are being tested to replace money completely.

3 The development of plastic money

The system has many advantages:

a. For customers
- Cards are convenient (no need to carry large sums of money around).
- Cards are safe thanks to their PIN.

b. For shops
- Cards favour impulse buying.
- They offer payment security.

CAN YOU ANSWER?

1. What are 'smart' credit cards?
2. Explain the limits and advantages of plastic money.

Words, words, words...

1

bank transfer: virement bancaire
bill of exchange: lettre de crédit
cash: liquide
draft: traite
means of payment: moyens de paiement

2

(bank) account: compte (en banque)
ATM (automatic teller machine): DAB (distributeur automatique de billets)
checkout: caisse de sortie
chip: puce
department store: grand magasin
to download: transférer
embedded: incrusté
issued: émis
PIN (personal identification number): code secret
purchase: achat
to record: enregistrer
smart card: carte à puce
wallet: portefeuille
to withdraw: (re)tirer (de l'argent)

3

convenient: pratique
impulse buying: achat par impulsion
safe: sans danger

Activities

❶ Vocabulaire

Complétez le texte à l'aide des mots proposés. Chaque mot ne peut servir qu'une fois, certains mots ne seront pas utilisés.

Liste de mots : *cash - chip - convenience - convenient - databases – dollars - downloaded - home shopping - impulse - means - network - pay - payment - PIN - purchases - purchasing - purse - smart card - stores - wallet.*

.... is developing quite fast today as more shoppers enjoy the .... of buying through their home phones or computers. To order via these ...., they have to pay with their ....

Companies can keep information about their customers and build useful ....

However, card .... is sometimes criticized as it favours .... buying and pushes people to live beyond their ....

New cards are being developed nowadays which may replace .... completely: users will have electronic .... with their .... and a pre-paid amount of money .... in a silicon ....

Thus, people will be able to pay for their daily .... with virtual money.

❷ Traduction

Traduisez les phrases ci-dessous en anglais.

– Les consommateurs ont changé : ils veulent des réductions sur tous leurs achats.

....

– Il y a beaucoup de produits jetables : c'est plus pratique.

....

– De nombreux magasins de bricolage ont ouvert en banlieue.

....

– À cause de la concurrence, les entreprises essaient de fidéliser leurs clients.

....

– Les cartes de paiement à puce sont plus sûres que les autres.

....

– La puce informatique incrustée dans le plastique contient des informations confidentielles sur l'utilisateur.

....

....

– Les enfants sont prescripteurs d'achat. C'est la raison pour laquelle il y a tant de publicités télévisées qui les ciblent.

....

....

3

❸ Travail de compréhension sur les titres ▶ **Survival kit**, p. 167

a. Lisez les titres suivants.

1. Has your credit card got a double?

2. Booming Ikea to slash its prices

3. British car buyers are still paying 52% more

4. Japanese Consumers Pull Back on Spending

5. Cost of online shopping spirals

6. Computer sales take a nosedive

7. London is among costliest cities

8. UK petrol prices worst in Europe

9. Shoppers spend £115bn a week

10. *Consumer Confidence Falls Again in Euro Zone*

11. Check out the nation's favourites

12. *U.S. Champagne Sales Go Flat*

b. Identifez, par un repérage couleur, les mots-clés des titres.

c. Les titres 2, 5, 7, 8 et 10 ne sont pas des énoncés complets sur le plan grammatical. Réécrivez-les en ajoutant les éléments syntaxiques qui manquent.

....

....

....

....

....

....

d. Lisez les douze articles. Indiquez pour chacun le numéro du titre correspondant.

A. London is the sixth most expensive city in the world and has become more pricey than the famously affluent locations of Geneva, Singapore and Paris.

Titre n° ☐

B. The cost of buying goods and services over the Internet is soaring as struggling dotcom firms desperately try to make a profit.

Titre n° ☐

C. Britain still has the most expensive petrol in Europe but compares more favourably when it comes to car hire, according to new figures.

Titre n° ☐

D. Scare stories about a recession are lost on the nation's shopaholics who are splashing out £115 billion a week.

Titre n° ☐

E. Tokyo – Japan retail sales slid for a third straight month in June, the government reported on Thursday.

Titre n° ☐

F. Furniture giant Ikea is cutting its prices by more than £26 million on the back of record sales figures.

Titre n° ☐

G. Ian Tolfts would love to visit Rio de Janeiro. So he was particularly surprised when he was told his credit card had already been there.

Titre n° ☐

H. Cars are up to 52 percent more expensive in Britain than anywhere else in Europe, the latest price survey reveals.

Titre n° ☐

I. Britain's shoppers are filling their trolleys with ready meals, junk food and increasing quantities of booze, according to a list of the 50 leading supermarket brands published yesterday by Marketing magazine.

Titre n° ☐

J. Personal computer sales in Britain have fallen for the first time since the IT revolution began.

Sales were down by 11.8 per cent in the past quarter. Sales to business also fell, by 4.9 per cent.

Experts blamed the fear of recession, the use of computers in offices and market saturation.

Titre n° ☐

K. BRUSSELS – Executives and consumers in the dozen countries sharing the euro currency became more pessimistic for the fifth straight month in June, figures showed Tuesday, as a slowing economy forced companies to cut production and to dismiss workers.

Titre n° ☐

L. NEW YORK. – Champagne, the effervescent drink of celebration that represents one-fifth of all French wine exports, is suffering from what could become a severe slump in the United States.

Titre n° ☐

e. Identifiez dans chaque article, par un repérage couleur, les mots-clés qui correspondent aux mots-clés de son titre.

❹ Questions en anglais

a. Explain who baby boomers are.

....

....

b. What are FMCGs? Give various examples.

....

....

c. What are disposables? Give various examples.

....

....

d. Make a list of store brands and famous icon brands.

....

....

❺ Analyse de graphiques

Survival kit, p. 185

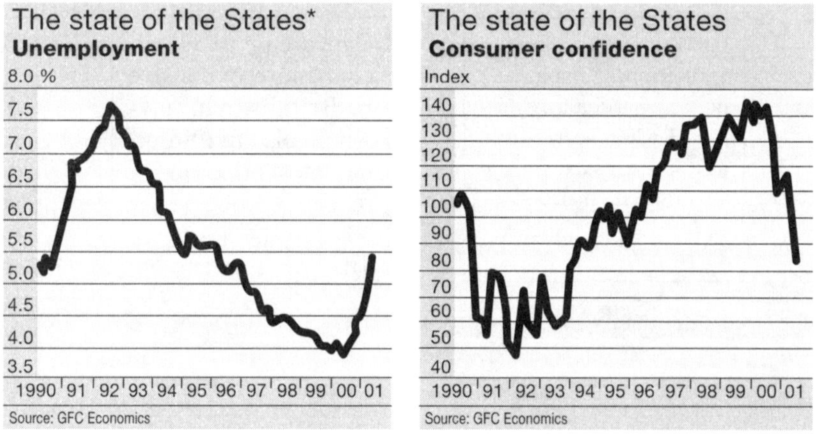

* The States: the USA.

The Guardian, November 14, 2001.

a. Faites un commentaire de ces deux graphiques en anglais, en insistant sur la complémentarité des deux évolutions.

– Utilisez les verbes suivants : *to represent, to skyrocket, to peak, to plummet, to reach a bottom low, to pick up, to fluctuate, to rise, to fall.*

– Utilisez les prépositions suivantes : *at, to, by, between..., and, since, for.*

– Attention aux temps utilisés (prétérit avec un passé daté, ou *present perfect* avec *for* ou *since*).

....

....

....

....

....

....

b. Expliquez le jeu de mots du titre.

....

....

Chapter 4. **Distribution**

1. The different types of outlets

1 Vending machines

They concern many products and services: automatic teller machines (ATMs) in banks, food, newspapers, cigarettes, etc.

a. Advantages
Quick return on investment, profitable in travel-related areas (stations, airports, hotels, cinemas).

b. Reasons accounting for their development
No staff, no overheads, round-the-clock sales.

c. Main drawbacks
Breakdowns and vandalism, necessity to adapt to new currencies.

2 Markets

They are held daily or weekly, in the high streets of city or town centres. All sorts of goods are sold: food, clothing, footwear, leather articles, books, pottery, etc.

a. Advantages
- Low prices because of low overheads.
- Fresh products when sold by the producer/farmer.

b. Drawbacks
Not always a good quality-price ratio if the goods are unsatisfactory.

3 Unit, or corner, shops/stores

They are small shops, situated near homes, away from main shopping centres.
They may sell a single kind of product (bread, meat, fish or vegetables) or they offer a large number of goods with a limited range in each (= convenience stores).
Convenience/neighbourhood stores are often family-owned, and run by minorities.

a. Advantages
These shops have long opening hours. They can be used by people who can't shop far away (no car, etc.), who have no time to go shopping, or to save a trip to a supermarket. They offer special services such as film processing and photocopies.

b. Main drawback
They generally sell at high prices.

4 Specialist shops

They deal in a restricted range of goods (cars, hi-fi, electrical goods, sports apparel, books, CDs and videos, cosmetics). They are often easily recognized because of their design: the layout is always the same.

Two main types

a. Licensed dealers
Many manufacturers, such as car manufacturers, use the services of licensed dealers/subcontractors who have the exclusive rights for the products.

b. Franchises
A franchise is an agreement between a franchisor (a large business, a brand name) and a franchisee (an individual entrepreneur).

The franchisee pays:
- a front-end/franchising fee to buy the right to operate a business,
- a percentage of the turnover to the franchisor (royalties).

And he gets in exchange:
- the brand and reputation,
- know-how and training,
- advertising campaigns.

Franchises are flourishing today:
- on the domestic market: franchising is a way to start up a business with little capital and experience and less risk,
- on foreign markets: franchising is a way to team up with local partners who know the marketplace.

But some franchisors impose standard-format stores, their own goods, global advertising campaigns, and they often oblige their franchisees to respect certain rules: dress-code, prices and opening hours, etc.

5 Department stores

Department stores are huge shops with many departments on several floors (Le Printemps in Paris, Harrod's in London, Macy's in New York, for example).

a. They went through a period of decline in the 1990s because:
- they are located in city centres, where parking is expensive,
- their prices were too high,
- they often had an old-fashioned image,
- customers preferred to shop in specialist stores for expertise and choice, or in hypermarkets for better value.

b. Nowadays, they are making profits again because:
- they concentrate their sales on upmarket, prestigious, fashionable brands,
- they have modernized their offer to satisfy their customers,
- they adapt to the clients they target (tourists, suburbans or locals).

6 Supermarkets and hypermarkets

Super and hypermarkets are located in suburbs, on the outskirts of cities, often in shopping malls/centres, which are becoming leisure-oriented places (with entertainment, restaurants, cinemas, banks, etc.). In those places, shoppers can experience 'fun shopping', also called 'retailtainment', and, of course, make purchases.

Reasons for their success

a. The consumers' new spending patterns
(See chapter 3 - Consumers, p. 132)

b. They offer:
- facilities (free car parks and comfortable one-stop indoor shopping),
- a very large range of goods (FMCGs, white and brown goods),
- a good quality-price ratio,
- long opening hours.

c. New techniques
Technology allows substantial economies of scale and improved service:
- the use of barcodes rationalizes stock management,
- scanning devices at check-outs or on trolley carts reduce queuing.

d. The influence of market studies
Super and hypermarkets use market studies to make people buy more:
- impulse buying: the various basic products are laid out in different aisles. Shoppers have to walk round in order to purchase the essential goods and buy other goods on impulse,
- strategic places: the products to be pushed/promoted are placed at eye-level, near the check-out to tempt shoppers when they queue or at the end of aisles.

7 Hard-discounters

They 'pile it high and sell it cheap', i.e. offer low prices thanks to:
- bulk purchases to obtain the best conditions with suppliers,
- reduced profit margins,
- low-price generics or store-brands,
- a minimum number of employees who do everything,
- warehouse-like shops.

8 Factory outlets/designer discount malls

They sell end-of-range items or outdated brands at reduced prices in shopping malls away from city centres.

9 Entertainment-oriented stores

a. Who? Famous brands (Nike, Disney, for example).

b. What? Many entertaining activities (multimedia games, video clips, cafés, jacuzzis, etc.), together with goods sold.

c. Goal: hope consumers will come back to shops, to have a good time and eventually to spend money.

CAN YOU ANSWER?

1. Why do neighbourhood shops have problems nowadays?
2. Explain the advantages and drawbacks of franchising.
3. What does 'fun shopping' consist in?
4. What are the main factors accounting for the success of supermarkets?
5. Would you say hard-discounting is a fad or will it last?

Words, words, words...

1

automatic teller machine (ATM): distributeur automatique de billets (DAB)
breakdown: panne
currency: devise
overheads: frais généraux
profitable: rentable
return on investment: rentabilité
round-the-clock: 24 heures sur 24
travel related area: zone de transit
vending machine: distributeur automatique

2

footwear: chaussures
leather: cuir
pottery: faïence

3

convenience store/unit/corner shop: magasin de proximité
opening hours: heures d'ouverture
range: choix
to save a trip: éviter un déplacement
to sell: vendre
shopping centre: centre commercial

4

advertising campaign: campagne de publicité
brand: marque
domestic market: marché national
exclusive rights: droits exclusifs
foreign markets: à l'étranger
franchise: franchise
franchisee: franchisé
franchisor: franchiseur
front-end/franchising fee: droit d'entrée
know-how: savoir-faire
layout: présentation
licensed dealer: concessionnaire
manufacturer: fabricant
marketplace: marché
range of goods: gamme de produits
right: le droit de
sports apparel: articles de sport
subcontractor: sous traitant
to team up with: travailler avec
training: formation
turnover: chiffre d'affaires

5

department: rayon
department store: grand magasin
floor: étage
local: personne qui habite à proximité
old-fashioned: démodé
suburban: banlieusard
to target: cibler
upmarket: haut de gamme
value (for money): bon rapport qualité-prix

6

aisle: allée de circulation
at eye-level: à hauteur des yeux
barcode: code-barres
check out: caisse
economies of scale: économies d'échelle
fun-shopping: acheter en s'amusant
impulse buying: achat par impulsion
indoor: à l'intérieur
to lay out: présenter
leisure: loisir
market study: étude de marché
outskirts: périphérie
pattern: modèle
purchase: achat
to queue (US: to stand in line): faire la queue
range: gamme
"retailtainment" (retail + entertainment): « divertivente »
scanning device: scanner
stock management: gestion du stock
suburb: banlieue
trolley cart: chariot

7

discounter: revendeur à marge réduite
generics: produits génériques
in bulk: en grosses quantités
profit margin: marge bénéficiaire
store-brand: marque de distributeur
supplier: fournisseur
warehouse: entrepôt

8

designer discount mall: centre (commercial) de déstockage de marques
end-of-range: fin de série
factory-outlet: magasin d'usine
outdated: démodé

9

entertainment-oriented store: magasin de « consommation-plaisir »

2. Home shopping

1 Mail-ordering

Firms operate from warehouses in low-rental areas, therefore have low overheads.

a. Advantages for consumers

– Very competitive prices.
– Savings in terms of time and transport: no opening hours, better service thanks to phone/fax/computer ordering, delivery times cut to one day.

b. Problems

Some consumers hesitate to buy from a catalogue, many goods are returned.

2 E-commerce (see chapter 6 p. 159)

a. Who sells on-line

– "Click" companies (or dot.coms), such as Amazon, or Dell computers.
– "Click and mortar" companies, i.e. ordinary firms (= "brick and mortar") such as Virgin, Toys'R Us, Tesco, Fnac or Gap, who have opened stores on line.

b. The best products

Computer goods, books, records, airline tickets, holidays and FMCGs.

c. Advantages

– For companies: the Net represents a new distribution channel.
– For consumers: they can surf and place orders worldwide, from home, at any time.

3 Television selling

Consumers order the goods they have seen on TV through a computer network or via a toll-free number.

4 Direct-to-home retailing

– Door-to-door selling for books, insurance, etc.
– Home parties (demonstrating products in a friendly atmosphere).

A seven-day cooling-off period law has been passed to protect consumers.

CAN YOU ANSWER?

1. Why is home-shopping developing?
2. Do you think e-commerce will become bigger and bigger? Why/why not?

Words, words, words...

1

delivery time: délai de livraison
home shopping: achats à domicile
low-rental: loyer bon marché
mail-ordering: vente par correspondance (VPC)
overheads: frais généraux
to return: renvoyer
savings: économies
warehouse: entrepôt

2

"brick and mortar" company: entreprise « physique », qui a « pignon sur rue »
"click and mortar" company: entreprise qui vend « sur rue et en ligne »
distribution channel: réseau de distribution
dot.com/click company: cyber-entreprise
e-commerce: commerce électronique/en ligne/cyber-commerce
on-line: en ligne, sur Internet
sales: ventes

3

network: réseau
toll-free number: numéro vert/gratuit

4

cooling-off period: période de réflexion
door-to-door: porte-à-porte
home party: vente à domicile
insurance: assurance

3. Retailing and the environment

1 Changes in the last twenty years

a. Opening in the suburbs

Hypermarkets, shopping malls and hard discounters have sprung up in suburbs, on the outskirts of big cities or towns (in France: Val d'Europe near Disneyland Paris; in the UK: the Metro Centre near Newcastle, Bluewater in Kent, Lakeside in Essex, Meadowhall near Sheffield; in the USA: the mall of America in Minnesota, the Redmond Town mall in the state of Washington; in Portugal the Vasco de Gama centre in Lisbon).

b. High street stores close

- City centres tend to become "food deserts" for the have-nots, the minorities, the people who have no car and who cannot afford a trip to shop in the suburbs.
- City centre shops close because of high rents, lack of shopping space, and shortage of car-parking areas.

2 Reactions

a. New rules

Shopping mall developers now have to prove that there is no suitable location inside a town before they can hope to get planning permission on another site.

b. Permits

They are difficult to obtain, due to:
- the suspension of the building of more malls in France and Great Britain,
- the desire to reduce pollution from car exhausts and traffic jams,
- conservation of suburban green spaces.

c. Charity shops

- In British high streets, charity shops have opened, such as Oxfam, Red Cross, Imperial Cancer, Relate (Marriage Guidance Council), Scope (cerebral palsy), Mind (Mental Health), PDSA (People's Dispensary for Sick Animals), Dr Barnardos (Children's Society), NSPCC (National society for the prevention of cruelty against children), Heart Foundation, etc.
- They sell second-hand articles and unwanted gifts: clothes, books, toys, china, crockery, bed-linen, curtains, saucepans.
- The Oxfam charity shops also sell fair-trade goods (tea, coffee, etc.) direct from the growers.
- Their running costs are low as their staff are mostly unpaid volunteers.

d. In-town shopping malls

- City centres are being renovated and transformed into popular shopping malls with plenty of shopping space, cinemas, bars and cafés (*cf.* in the UK: Eldon Square in Newcastle, the Oracle mall in Reading, the West Quay in Southampton, Merry Hill centre near Birmingham).
- Pedestrian precincts are being developed.
- Car parks are enlarged and modernized.
- Safety is increased, shop-lifting is reduced with the introduction of cameras.
- Public transport is improved.

3 Sunday shopping

- In Germany, Denmark, Greece, and Holland: strict regulations against Sunday shopping.
- In France and Italy: Sunday trading is allowed in tourist areas.
- In Ireland and Portugal: shops can open whenever they wish to.
- In Spain, a 1996 trading law forbids the opening of stores on Sundays and public holidays.
- In Britain, a 1994 law allows the opening of small shops at any time, and the opening of large shops and supermarkets between 11 am and 5 pm on Sundays, and some hypermarkets can open 24 hours a day.
- In the USA, shopping is legal 24 hours a day, 7 days a week.

Opinions are divided.

a. Against
- Unions fear workers will have to work on Sundays without extra pay.
- Small shop-owners are afraid they will not be able to face the cost of Sunday double pay.
- Church officials claim that Sunday shopping is a danger to family life and social relationships.

b. For
- Families welcome the opportunity to do their shopping whenever they like.
- Store-owners can develop flexible working hours and increase profitability.
- Some employees welcome part-time jobs.

CAN YOU ANSWER?

1. What are the consequences of the retailing evolution on the environment and cities?
2. How do communities react?
3. Are you in favour of Sunday shopping?
4. Do you think the liberalization of shopping hours will make people consume more?

Words, words, words...

1

to afford: avoir les moyens de payer
have-nots: les pauvres
high street: rue commerçante
rent: loyer

2

bed linen : drap et taies d'oreiller
charity shop: magasin dont les bénéfices vont à une œuvre caritative
china: porcelaine
crockery: vaisselle
curtains : rideaux
developer: promoteur
exhaust: échappement
fair-trade : commerce équitable
freezing : gel
gift: cadeau
health : santé
heart : cœur
palsy : paralysie
pedestrian precinct : zone piétonne
permit: permis
rule: règle
safety: sécurité
saucepan : casserole
second-hand: d'occasion
shop lifting: vol à l'étalage
suburban: en banlieue
suitable: adapté
traffic jam: embouteillage

3

extra pay: salaire en plus
part-time job: emploi à temps partiel
profitability: rentabilité
shop/store-owner: petit commerçant
shopping hours: heures d'ouverture des magasins
(trade) union: syndicat
worker: employé

Activities

1 Analyse d'un dessin

a. Describe the franchising couple: what do the franchisor and the franchisee bring in the relationship?

....

....

....

b. What do they exchange as they get married?

....

c. What are the advantages and the risks for each party?

....

....

....

d. Would you like to become a franchisee? Why/why not?

....

....

2 Vocabulaire

Complétez le texte suivant avec les mots proposés. Chaque mot ne peut servir qu'une fois.

Liste de mots : *lady – place orders – e-mailing – door-to-door – directly – on line – sales representative – personal – customer.*

The Avon .... is still calling, but she's not going ...., she's .... Customers will soon be able to go to Avon Products Inc. .... and be directed to a sales representative in their area. They will be able to .... anytime and have the products shipped .... to them. The .... can send .... messages to each ....

4

❸ **Travail de compréhension sur les titres** ▶ **Survival kit**, p. 167

a. Lisez les titres suivants.

1. **Tesco is worth stockpiling**

2. Instant scanning system will price trolley full of shopping in seconds

3. **Half of shopkeepers suffer violent crime**

4. The "virtual Tesco"

5. **Women "bored with shopping"**

6. **M&S clothes sales fall again**

7. **Avon calling – in cyberspace**

8. **Kilos break human rights says grocer**

9. **Marks & Spencer Sales Rise**

10. **U.S. Schools Are Adding a 4th "R" to Curriculum: Retail**

b. Identifiez, par un repérage couleur, les mots-clés des titres.

c. Les titres 2, 3, 5, 7, 8 et 10 ne sont pas des énoncés complets sur le plan grammatical. Réécrivez-les en ajoutant les éléments syntaxiques qui manquent.

....

....

....

....

d. Lisez les dix articles. Indiquez pour chacun le numéro du titre correspondant.

A. The days of the supermarket check-out may be numbered. A British company is perfecting a machine for pricing shopping without removing items from a basket or trolley.

Titre n° ☐

B. Tesco is introducing "virtual" shop assistants to help take some of the stress out of shopping.

Titre n° ☐

C. Women say they are bored with shopping for clothes, according to a new report.

Titre n° ☐

D. Retailer Marks & Spencer is facing another blow this week when it will be forced to admit that sales in its core clothing division have fallen further. Insiders said that chairman Luc Vandevelde would have to tell shareholders at Wednesday's annual meeting that the latest womenswear collection has failed to please shoppers.

Titre n° ☐

E. Whatever happens, we will have to eat. No wonder that supermarket chains, alongside missile makers, have been flavour of the week on the Stock Exchange since the terrorists struck.

Titre n° ☐

F. Avon ladies will call on a new address this week – on the Internet. The cosmetics firm – famed for its "Avon calling" slogan – has a new website aimed at giving its mostly self-employed 160,000 UK staff all the latest product information.

Titre n° ☐

G. Being forced to sell fruit and veg in kilos rather than pounds and ounces breached human rights, a grocer yesterday told a court.

Titre n° ☐

H. Shopkeepers are increasingly the victims of violent crime, according to new figures. A survey shows that almost half of all independent retailers say they have been attacked – nearly double the rate last year.

Titre n° ☐

I. New York – From exclusive soft-drink contracts to computers displaying continuous advertising, corporate marketing in public schools is rising sharply.

Titre n° ☐

J. London – Marks & Spencer PLC on Tuesday reported its first quarterly sales increase in three years, sending its share price to a 20-month high.

Titre n° ☐

e. Identifiez dans chaque article, par un repérage couleur, les mots-clés qui correspondent aux mots-clés de son titre.

❹ Traduction

Traduisez les phrases ci-dessous en anglais.

– De nombreuses formes de commerce sont apparues à la fin des années 1990 grâce à l'informatique.

....

– Les supermarchés ont de plus en plus de succès, particulièrement quand ils sont situés dans un centre commercial.

....

....

– Les commerces de proximité sont pratiques car ils sont ouverts tard le soir.

....

– Le franchisé doit verser au franchiseur des royalties, c'est-à-dire un pourcentage sur son chiffre d'affaires.

....

....

– Les centres commerciaux deviennent des centres de loisirs qui attirent les clients grâce au nouveau concept de la « divertivente ».

....

....

– Les études en mercatique ont montré que les consommateurs sont plus susceptibles d'acheter des produits qui se trouvent à hauteur de l'œil.

....

....

– Les appareils pour lire les codes-barres ont permis de réduire le temps passé à faire la queue aux caisses de sortie.

....

....

– Les revendeurs à marge réduite achètent en grosses quantités pour obtenir les meilleurs prix avec leurs fournisseurs.

....

....

– Les magasins-entrepôts vendent des fins de série à prix réduits, mais les clients font-ils toujours vraiment de bonnes affaires ?

....

....

– Les syndicats sont opposés à l'ouverture des magasins le dimanche, car ils craignent que les employés soient obligés de travailler plus sans salaire supplémentaire.

....

....

....

Chapter 5. The environment

1. The characteristics of our environment today

1 A gap between rich and poor countries in the world, between over and under-populated countries

a. Rich/industrialized countries: the USA, Western Europe, Japan.
- They are characterized by low birth-rates and an ageing population.
- They pollute and waste.

b. Poor/developing countries: South America, Eastern Europe, Asia and Africa.
- They are characterized by exponentially growing populations, high birth-rates (apart from China where births are controlled by law) and a 'young' population.
- They are desperate to develop economically.

2 The globalization of exchanges

It implies more transport by road, air, sea and rail, and more tourism.

3 Urbanization

It causes deforestation and desertification in developing countries.
It transforms landscapes in industrialized countries (cutting down hedges and trees, building roads, housing estates, high-speed train lines and concrete surfaces for shopping malls and hypermarkets).

4 Industrialization of farming and fishing

a. Industrial farming
To make more profits, farmers, helped by European subsidies, have increased productivity, raising cattle and poultry in batteries.

b. Fish farms
Because of over-fishing in the North sea and a shortage of salmon, cod, whiting, herring and other wild species, fish farms have been set up.

5 Breakthroughs in biotechnology

Researchers are creating bio-engineered/transgenic/genetically engineered crops which can reduce the need for repeated spraying of insecticides and herbicides. This process has been applied to numerous types of produce.

CAN YOU ANSWER?
1. What opposes rich and poor countries in the world?
2. What has changed in agriculture and fishing recently?

5

Words, words, words...

1
ageing: vieillissant
birth-rate: taux de natalité
gap: fossé
to waste: gaspiller

3
concrete: béton
hedge: haie
high-speed train: train à grande vitesse (TGV)
housing estate: lotissement
landscape: paysage

4
cattle: bétail
cod: cabillaud/morue
fish farm: établissement piscicole
herring: hareng
poultry: volaille
to raise: élever
salmon: saumon
species: espèce
whiting: merlan

5
bio-engineered/transgenic/genetically engineered: génétiquement modifié
breakthrough: découverte
produce: produits agricoles
spraying: pulvérisation

2. Consequences: environmental problems

1 Warming of the planet

a. Facts

- Worldwide temperatures have increased by 6% over the last century.
- The climate is changing with extreme weather more often: unusual periods of dry and hot weather creating droughts, heavy rain, storms and hurricanes causing floods.
- Water is becoming scarce in lots of countries.

b. Reasons

- Factories, power plants, automobiles and farms belch out toxic gases - carbon mono/dioxide and methane - into the atmosphere.
- Toxic emissions are trapped and it creates a greenhouse effect over cities.
- Ozone spreads as the sun heats the toxic gases.
- Acid rain kills trees and erodes the soil.

2 Pollution

a. Of the ground by:

- pesticides, fertilizers, agro-industrial waste and nuclear toxic waste.
- domestic rubbish (plastics, packaging, glass bottles and batteries).

b. Of the air by:

- smokestacks and the use of CFC, for air-conditioning,
- the burning of fossil fuels (car exhausts and central heating systems),
- radioactive leaks and waste and the use of asbestos in buildings.

c. Of water by:

- chemicals (lead, nitrates), oil slicks and agro-industrial sewage.

3 Extinction of species

- Some species (animals and plants) have disappeared everywhere in the world.
- Millions are doomed to extinction in the near future.
- As half of the medicines are found in nature, we are killing the cures for future diseases.

4 Epidemics, new diseases and viruses

- Animals are regularly infected by diseases on a global level.

CAN YOU ANSWER?

1. Why are temperatures rising?
2. What causes pollution?
3. What are the consequences of animal and vegetal extinction?

Words, words, words...

1

to belch out: vomir
drought: sécheresse
flood: inondation
greenhouse effect: effet de serre
to heat: réchauffer
hurricane: ouragan
power plant: centrale
scarce: rare
soil: terre
storm: tempête
trapped: coincé
warming: réchauffement

2

asbestos: amiante
battery: pile
central heating: chauffage central
CFCs: chloro-fluoro-carbones
domestic rubbish: ordures ménagères
exhaust: échappement
fossil fuels (oil, coal, gas): combustibles fossiles (pétrole, charbon, gaz)
ground: sol
lead: plomb
leak: fuite
oil slick: marée noire
sewage: eaux usées
smokestacks: cheminées d'usine

3

cure: remède
disease: maladie
doomed: condammé
medicine: médicament

3. Reactions to environmental issues

1 Laws and controls

– The 1992 Rio summit and the 1997 Kyoto protocol called on industrialized nations to reduce carbon dioxide (CO_2) emissions causing the greenhouse effect.
– Clean air acts were passed by European governments in the 1980s and by the US as from 2006, and eco-labels were adopted to develop recycling.
– Catalytic converters, lead-free/unleaded petrol/gas(oline) were introduced.
– Fishing quotas, regulations, and directives to reduce waste have been imposed by the EU.
– Compulsory labels were introduced for genetically altered products.

2 New mentalities

a. Consumers
They take initiatives to conserve energy (sorting and recycling their domestic rubbish).

b. Governments and associations
– In Europe, green parties influence policies.
– In Anglo-Saxon countries, religious groups and charities, green lobbies and associations such as Greenpeace, Friends of the Earth and the WWF are very active.

c. Companies
– They adopt eco-friendly, corporate-citizen policies.
– They emphasize what they do to reuse and recycle products.
– They put money back into their communities.

3 Development of new energies and new forms of transport

– Renewable energies are developed (solar, hydro and wind energy) and bio-fuels are introduced to replace petrol and diesel-oil in cars, trucks and tractors.
– Electric transport is promoted in cities.

4 New products

a. Organic food
– More and more people switch to natural products and become vegetarians.
– Britain's organic food market has grown six-fold since 1990.
– One third of the French regularly buy organic products.
– Organic products are now sold in hypermarket chains all over the world.

b. Farming is becoming reasonable.
Farmers accept strict controls by government bodies.

CAN YOU ANSWER?

1. What has changed in people's mentalities towards the environment?
2. Has this entailed changes in our everyday life and in our buying patterns?
3. How do companies show they feel concerned?

5

Words, words, words...

1

catalytic converter: pot catalytique
compulsory: obligatoire
eco-label: écolabel
government agency/body: secrétariat d'État/ministère
issue: problème
lead-free/unleaded: sans plomb
petrol (GB)/gasoline (US): essence

2

charity: association caritative
corporate citizen: entreprise citoyenne
eco-friendly: écologique
lobby: groupe de pression
to sort: trier

3

bio-fuel: biocarburant
diesel-oil: gazole
renewable: renouvelable
solar/hydro/wind energy: énergie solaire/hydroélectrique/éolienne

4

to grow six-fold: être six fois plus important
organic food/products: aliments/produits bio(logiques)
reasonable farming: agriculture raisonnée

4. The environmental issue today

1 Limits

a. In industrialized countries

– As regulations are very strict and costly, they favour big companies at the expense of smaller ones.

– Opponents to environmental action lobby in Washington, D.C. and in Brussels, and, as a result, international conferences trying to reduce pollution often fail.

– Organic products are more expensive to make, and consumers are asked to pay a tax to finance the cost of recycling discarded high tech equipment, household goods, toys, etc. hence higher retailing prices.

– Producing bio-fuels requires fossil energy, contributes to greenhouse effects and may take up land needed for food crops.

b. In developing countries

– Officials say they will develop their economies without caring about the environment, unless rich countries help them with funds.

– The situation of post-Communist Central and Eastern Europe is catastrophic as regards the environment.

2 Perspectives

Our planet needs joint action with the help of the media to publicize events.

a. More laws

– To develop birth control and contraception in developing countries.

– To limit car traffic, to impose speed limits and the use of public transport.

– To impose taxes and recycling on households and companies on the amount of garbage produced with the principle of polluter-payer.

– To impose stricter labelling and traceability on the food we buy.

b. Government action

– Locally, in each community, each country, imposing cleaner fuel and the sorting of rubbish.

– On an international level, at global climate conferences with other environmental and energy ministers from around the world: the goal being to impose global policies to combat climate change in the next century, before it is too late!

c. Education

– At school, in the media, in public awareness campaigns.

People must feel concerned by what is going on in their communities, on their planet, for themselves and for their children's future.

CAN YOU ANSWER?

1. What limits consumers' purchases of organic products?
2. Are laws the only solution?

Words, words, words...

1

costly: onéreux
crop: récolte
discarded: au rebut
to fail: échouer
fund: fonds
household goods: électroménager
to lobby: faire pression
regulation: réglementation
retailing price: prix au détail

2

car traffic: circulation automobile
dual: double
garbage: ordures
household: foyer
labelling: étiquetage
law: loi
public awareness campaign: campagne de sensibilisation
rubbish: ordures
speed limit: vitesse limite
tax: impôt

Activities

❶ Vrai ou faux ?

Après avoir étudié le cours pp. 149-152, dites si ces énoncés sont vrais ou faux. Quand ils sont faux, corrigez-les.

– Developing countries are characterized by a low birth-rate.

....

– Industrial farming has reduced productivity.

....

– Breakthroughs in biotechnology have no consequences on human health.

....

– With transgenic products, farmers can reduce the use of pesticides.

....

– Fish farms have been set up because there are too many fish in the North Sea.

....

– Pollution affects the ground, the air and water.

....

– Temperatures are higher nowadays than they were in the 19th century.

....

– Oil slicks pollute the air.

....

– With the extinction of species, we reduce our chances of finding new medicines in nature's eco-systems.

....

– The environment became a global issue after the Second World War.

....

– New regulations aimed at reducing the greenhouse effect are currently being implemented in industrialized countries.

....

– Sales of organic products are very limited.

....

– Fewer and fewer people become vegetarians.

....

– Companies do not include the environment in their corporate-citizen attitudes.

....

– Developing countries are ready to face environmental regulations.

....

❷ Travail de compréhension sur les titres ▶ **Survival kit,** p. 167

a. Lisez les titres suivants.

1. **Deal rescues Kyoto treaty**

2. **Earth warming faster than ever, say experts**

3. **McDonald's hit by food scares**

4. Amazon may be a desert in 100 years

5. ***Insurance For Changes In Weather***

6. ***Biotech Crops Moving Fast Around Globe***

b. Identifiez, par un repérage couleur, les mots-clés des titres.

c. Tous les titres ne sont pas des énoncés complets sur le plan grammatical. Réécrivez-les en ajoutant les éléments syntaxiques qui manquent.

....

....

....

....

....

....

d. Lisez les huit articles. Indiquez pour chacun le numéro du titre correspondant.

A.

The planet is warming even faster than climate experts feared, scientists warned yesterday.

They said temperatures were rising more quickly than at any time in the past 1,000 years, putting millions of people at risk of catastrophes.

Titre n° ☐

B.

Washington – After two unusually warm winters melted profits at his natural gas distributing company in Dallas, Robert Best decided he needed protection. So he spent $4.9 million on a new tool called weather insurance.

Titre n° ☐

C.

A historic deal to tackle global warming was agreed by 178 nations yesterday.

The compromise – reached after 48 hours of intensive talks in Bonn – means the 1997 Kyoto treaty to reduce greenhouse gases will soon come into force.

Titre n° ☐

D.

Consumer fears over CJD and foot and mouth have led to a slump in profits at fast food chain.

Titre n° ☐

E.

Marks & Spencer and Somerfield were yesterday "named and shamed" by Friends of the Earth for the levels of pesticide residues on their fruit and vegetables. The environmental campaign group claimed M&S was the worst offender, with 63 per cent of its produce containing residues.

Titre n° ☐

F.

Within a century the world's weather could be turned on its head, covering the Sahara in thick forest and making the Amazon a barren desert, it was claimed yesterday.

Titre n° ☐

G.

Organic food is the safer and better option for healthy eating, producers claimed yesterday.

People who want to improve their intake of minerals and vitamin C and reduce exposure to harmful pesticides and additives should choose organic if possible, the Soil Association said.

Titre n° ☐

H.

Chicago – Despite persistent concerns about genetically modified crops, they are spreading so rapidly that it has become almost impossible for consumers to avoid them, agriculture experts say.

Titre n° ☐

5

e. Identifiez dans chaque article, par un repérage couleur, les mots-clés qui correspondent aux mots-clés de son titre.

f. Trouvez des titres pour les articles qui n'en ont pas.

....

....

....

....

❸ Analyse de texte

WE'VE WON AN AWARD!

Road congestion is a growing environmental issue, which is why we've been making more use of trains – and it's earned us a Queen's Award for Enterprise. Last year, we cut down on 5,528 road journeys and 537,745 litres of diesel. Now we've been given a grant to convert 40 more of our trucks from diesel to gas – a cleaner fuel that reduces carbon monoxide levels by 99 per cent.

Safeway Magazine, July 2001.

award: récompense
issue: problème
grant: bourse

The Safeway stores are a British hypermarket chain.

a. In what way does Safeway show it is concerned by environmental issues?

b. How was it rewarded in 2001 for its commitment?

c. Why does the company feel the need to inform its customers in the *Safeway Magazine*?

❹ Analyse de graphiques

Survival kit, p. 185

Going Organic

The mad-cow epidemic is propelling changes in Europe's landscape and diet.

Organic agriculture in the EU
in millions of hectares

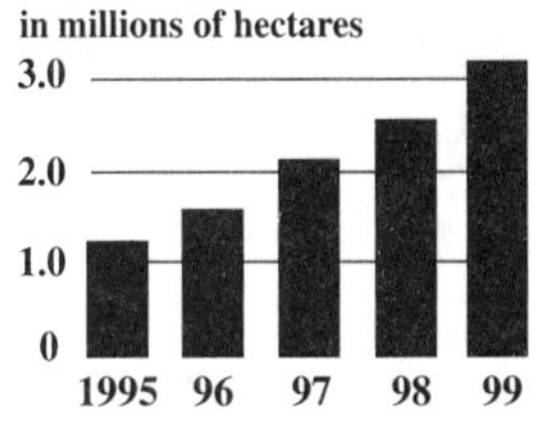

EU: Farms organic three times more than North Amecica
France: Organic farm-land increased by 200% since '95

Beef consumption*

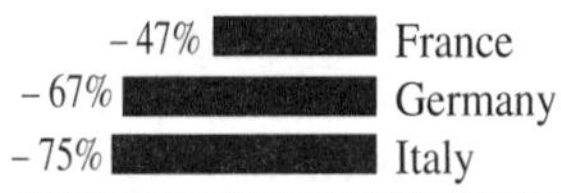

*FRANCE, '95-'00: GERMAN Y, '99-'00: ITALY, END OF '00
SOURCES: NEWSWEEK REPORTING

Newsweek, February 26, 2001.

a. How has organic agriculture evolved since 1995?

b. What has recently changed in people's consumption of beef in France, Germany and Italy?

Chapter 6. The new technologies

1. Computer technology is developing

1 Digital information is everywhere

– Data, files, videos and music can now be exchanged via e-mail or downloaded onto a computer from a website.
– Computer users can transfer songs from a CD onto an MP3 player.
– Data files can be transferred from one computer to another using a flash drive or USB key.
– The documents which are sent by e-mail, downloaded or transported lose no quality when they are duplicated/cloned because they are digital.

2 People can buy powerful and user-friendly equipment

– Digital equipment has become progressively more compact and user-friendly.
– Desktop computers are equiped with wide flat-panel screens.
– Mobile lightweight computers (palmtop, tablet/pocket PCs, notebooks and PDAs) are also developing, sold with powerful batteries.
– Most computers, including laptops, come equipped with built-in CD-ROM and DVD burners, allowing the user to manipulate large amounts of data and to work easier and faster with audio and video files.
– Data can be stored on internal and external hard drives, flash drives/USB keys, CDs and DVDs.

3 Costs are falling

– The price of hardware and software equipment regularly declines, thanks to the miniaturisation of components, and to the outsourcing of production in countries where labour costs are low.
– Computer and software companies manufacture very similar products which cannot differentiate themselves easily from competitors. In consequence, products such as digital cameras, web-cams, scanners, printers, copiers, DVD recorders, PCs and digital music instruments have become cheap commodities, low-margin products which people buy on price only.
– Freeware services are provided on the Web.
– The cost of phone service itself is plummeting as companies provide nearly free phone services together with broadband delivery of the Internet.

CAN YOU ANSWER?

1. What has changed in digital equipment recently?
2. Why does the price of digital equipment regularly decline?

Words, words, words...

1

data: données
digital: numérique
to download: télécharger
to duplicate/to clone: copier
file: fichier
MP3 player: lecteur MP3
website: site Internet

2

battery: pile
burner: graveur
desktop computer: ordinateur de bureau
drive: mémoire/disque
flat panel: écran plat
laptop: ordinateur portable
lightweight: léger
pocket/palmtop/notebook/ Personal Data Assistant: ordinateur de poche
ROM (Read Only Memory): mémoire morte
user-friendly: convivial
wide screen: écran large

3

broadband: haut débit
commodity: marchandise
component: composant
digital camera: appareil photo numérique
freeware: logiciel libre
low-margin: à marge réduite
to outsource: externaliser
to plummet: chuter
printer: imprimante
recorder: enregistreur
software: logiciel

2. Interactive exchanges invade the world

1 Different types of messages are available

a. Audio messages
- Telephone exchanges, streaming radio, VOIP computers.
- Podcasts, radio broadcasts and MP3 files, downloaded on websites.

b. Written messages
- SMS, MMS (called "instant messaging" or "IMing" in the USA).
- Web pages.
- E-mails messages and attachments to them (word processing, spreadsheet files, etc.).

c. Visual messages
- TV programs, videos, photos and films.
- GPS mapping instructions, and aerial maps.

2 The messages are broadcast through different networks

a. Through the World Wide Web, also called the Internet, a global network of computers which can communicate with one another
- About 60% of households in industrialised countries are connected, more and more often by Wi-Fi.
- To be connected, you need a computer, a telephone line, a modem or Ethernet connections, and an account with an ISP (Internet Service Provider).
- When you subscribe, you are given a secret password and an Internet address which enable you to log on the Net.
- Search engines give access to databases or to information on everything: books, job offers, leisure activities, finance, travel, etc.

b. Through national networks
- Traditional phone lines provide narrow band connections and faster broadband connections with ADSL (Asymmetric Digital Subscriber Line).
- Cellular phones offer UMTS (Universal Mobile Telecommunication System) connections.
- Fibre optic cables allow the transmission of information at the fastest speed of all.
- Satellites broadcast information to dishes.

c. Through local networks
- LANs (Local Area Networks), or Intranet servers, based either on Ethernet or on Wi-Fi technology, are used in local 'hot-zones', in companies, airports, stations, hospitals, universities and city-districts.

CAN YOU ANSWER?
1. Which types of messages are available?
2. How are the messages broadcast?

Words, words, words...

1

attachment: pièce jointe
device: dispositif
GPS (Global Positioning System): système mondial de localisation
ISP: fournisseur d'accès
MMS (Multimedia Message Service): service d'échanges multimédia
networked: en réseau
SMS (Short Message Service): texto
spreadsheet: tableau
streaming: en continu
VOIP (Voice Over Internet Protocol): téléphone branché sur ordinateur
word processing: traitement de texte

2

to broadcast: transmettre
cellular phone: téléphone mobile/portable
current events: actualité
dish: antenne parabolique
hot-zone: zone équipée avec WI-FI
to log on: se connecter
narrow band: bas débit
password: mot de passe
real estate: immobilier
search engine: moteur de recherche
to subscribe: s'abonner

3. The world we live in has changed

1 New companies have been created

– Some are small start-up companies, also called dot coms (.coms). Others such as Microsoft, Google, Yahoo, AOL, eBay and Dell have become giant companies.
– These firms are specialized in the manufacturing of hardware, software and micro-chips, in logistics, in consulting and support/after-sale services.

2 Three types of companies have emerged

– The "brick and mortar firms", also called "physical" companies, which operate in the traditional way from office buildings or store fronts.
– The virtual "click" companies, which operate on the net only (Amazon.com).
– The "click and mortar" companies, traditional "brick and mortar" which open e-commerce sites on the web, while still selling from their high-street/main street stores (Gap, Toys'R'Us, Tesco, etc.).

3 Several types of exchanges have developed

– B2A (Business to Administration), also called B2G (Business to Government), concerns relations between governments and companies.
– B2B (Business to Business) concerns commerce between companies.
– B2C (Business to Consumer) and C2C (Consumer to Consumer) concerns transactions between companies and consumers, and sales between individuals.
– P2P (Peer to Peer) concerns exchanges of files between individuals.

4 Our everyday life is changing

a. There are changes at work

– Companies hire staff online, and sometimes lay them off by e-mail or by SMS!
– Multinationals develop videoconferencing to reduce travel costs and to encourage teamwork on a global scale.
– Employees send and receive e-mails at work, and training is often organised online.
– New technologies have made tele-working and home-working possible.
– Companies use their site to project a positive image of themselves.

b. There are changes in our everyday life

– Central heating and alarm devices can be monitored at a distance.
– People shop online with e-commerce.
– They watch TV on computer screens, on mobile phones or MP3 players.
– Music and all sorts of documents are downloaded from Internet sites.
– Teenagers play games on their play-stations, on TV and computer screens.
– We communicate with relatives, friends or people we don't know by e-mail, in chat-rooms, on blogs, by SMS, in the street, at work, from home or in cyber-cafés.

5 New words have been coined: teleworking, telecommuting, on-line, on the web, e-commerce, e-trade, e-tailing, e-ducation, e-training, e-revolution, m-shopping, web-grocers, netizens, netiquette, to google, e-mail, webaholics, podcast, blog, chat, etc.

CAN YOU ANSWER?

1. What has changed in our everyday life?
2. Are new technologies always positive at work?

Words, words, words...

1

start-up/dot com/.com company: entreprise sur Internet
support/after-sale: après-vente

3

P2P: poste à poste / égal à égal

4

heating: chauffage

5

blog: site d'expression
chat: site de conversation
e-: en ligne
m- (= mobile): avec son téléphone portable
netiquette: règles de bienséance
netizen: internaute
tele-working/commuting: travail à distance
webaholic: mordu du web

4. The problems related to Information Technology

1 Control of information

It is impossible to control information on the web, hence the development of cyber-criminality with paedophile and pornographic sites.

2 Pirates and hackers

– Computers are often contaminated by bugs, viruses, worms and Trojans which can destroy hard-disc drives. A protection with fire-walls and anti virus software is necessary.
– “Spams” (unsolicited e-mail messages) can jam people’s in-boxes.
– It is impossible to be sure card payments are safe on the net, and users have to beware of hackers going “phishing” for data on their bank accounts.

3 Job cuts

Face to face jobs in travel agencies and stores are likely to disappear as companies move their businesses online and outsource services abroad.

4 Too much information

There is a risk of information overload, hence the need to check the accuracy of the data.

5 Risk of addiction

Spending time on the Internet can develop into an obsession. Webaholics become addicted to video games and to surfing on the net, risking obesity if they stop participating in sports.

6 Risk of marginalization

As time goes by, people who are not comfortable with computers risk becoming completely left out and isolated in this new digital society.

CAN YOU ANSWER?

1. Do you always feel safe on the net? Why?
2. Who may become marginalized in this new digital society?

Words, words, words...

2

fire-wall: pare-feu
hacker: pirate informatique
in-box: boîte de réception
to jam: bloquer
“phishing”: piratage de données bancaires (*cf.* to fish !)
software: logiciel
spam: message indésirable/pourriel
worm/Trojan: virus

4

accuracy: exactitude
overload: surcharge

5

addiction: dépendance

Activities

1 Vocabulaire

Complétez le texte à l'aide des mots proposés.

Liste de mots : *work - computer (2) - broadband (2) - low-income - rise - success - years - software - access - training - Internet - euro - home - online.*

Computers for all

Currently 50% of French households have a ...., but most .... families do not. As from next January, they will have the chance to have a ...., complete with ...., ... internet ...., and home .... for only 1 .... a day for 3 ....

The desire to see more people both at .... and at .... using the .... is a key part of plans to see more government services delivered .... and to provide .... to all parts of the country.

The move follows the .... of a similar scheme for students which saw their computer usage .... immediately from 8 to 29%.

2 Questions en anglais

a. How do companies use information technology?

....

....

....

b. How do individuals use information technology?

....

....

....

c. Can you connect online when you are away from home or from the office? How?

....

....

....

d. Does the revolution in information technology create or suppress jobs?

....

....

....

e. How long do you spend online everyday? Are you a webaholic? Could you live without a computer? Without a mobile phone? Justify your answer.

....

....

....

❸ **Travail de compréhension sur les titres**

a. Lisez les titres suivants.

1. **BT to offer broadband up to 8MB**

2. **Tesco to sell tables and chairs online**

3. **Clicks, bricks and bargains**

4. **Parents warned of webcam danger**

5. China's wild web

6. **California town up for sale on eBay for £1m**

7. **Christmas presents power boom in music downloads**

8. **Computer help offered for the older surfers**

9. **Software by Google is aimed at Microsoft**

b. Identifiez, par un repérage couleur, les mots-clés des titres.

c. Les titres ne sont pas des énoncés complets sur le plan grammatical. Réécrivez-les en ajoutant les éléments syntaxiques qui manquent.

....

....

....

....

....

....

....

....

....

d. Lisez les dix articles. Inscrivez pour chacun le numéro du titre correspondant.

A.

Despite concerns about a fall in consumer confidence, online purchases on websites run by conventional retailers – once considered dinosaurs of the brick-and-mortar age – are growing the fastest.

Titre n° ☐

B.

By some estimates, there are more that 30,000 people patrolling the Web in China as Wild West capitalism, crime, piracy, pornography and other problems of the real economy in China have moved into the virtual one.

Titre n° ☐

C.

BT announced plans yesterday to massively increase the speed of the nation's broadband Internet access, paving the way for its autumn launch of a video-on demand service in conjonction with the digital terrestrial broadcaster Freeview.

Titre n° ☐

D.

Parents are being warned against letting children have webcams in their bedrooms after the arrest of a Canadian accused of tricking British girls into performing sex acts for him to watch over the Internet.

Titre n° ☐

E.

Holidaymakers are being offered the opportunity to book flights or packages via a few clicks on a mobile phone with more than 25 budget airlines and several tour operators.

Titre n° ☐

F.

Sales of digital music rocketed in the week after Christmas, with British consumers downloading a record 1 million tracks to their new portable music players.

Titre n° ☐

G.

Tesco is considering selling furniture online next year in a move that would place it in direct competition with other rival retailers.

Titre n° ☐

H.

Further extending its efforts to areas beyond search technology, Google was set to announce Monday that it would offer software providing a range of online services for business users.

Titre n° ☐

I.

Looking for somewhere quiet? Bridgeville might be just the place. It has no shops, no cafés, one two-lane road and very few people. And it's to be sold on the online auction site e-Bay. Bids are invited, starting at $1.75m (£1m).

Titre n° ☐

J.

A French government project to promote computer use and the Internet amongst older people and the less well off has been launched. The new service provides details of special deals on computers, Internet access and training.

Titre n° ☐

e. Identifiez dans chaque article, par un repérage couleur, les mots-clés qui correspondent aux mots-clés de son titre.

f. Identifiez dans chaque article les autres informations contenues dans le paragraphe.

g. Trouvez un titre pour l'article qui n'en a pas.

....

....

❹ Traduction

Traduisez les phrases ci-dessous en anglais.

– Aujourd'hui, les gens communiquent plus facilement avec leur famille, leurs amis et avec des inconnus grâce à la révolution numérique.

....

....

....

– Les ordinateurs de bureau sont devenus des portables plus pratiques pour les utilisateurs.

....

....

– Les consommateurs peuvent acheter des appareils photos numériques et des caméras à des prix abordables dans des magasins ou bien sur les sites d'entreprises virtuelles.

....

....

....

– L'Internet est un réseau mondial d'ordinateurs qui peuvent communiquer entre eux.

....

....

– Le haut débit permet de télécharger plus de données en moins de temps.

....

....

– Les moteurs de recherche donnent accès à des bases de données sur d'innombrables sujets.

....

....

– Les nouvelles technologies ont rendu possibles le travail à distance et le commerce en ligne.

....

....

– De nouvelles entreprises se sont spécialisées dans la vente de matériel, de logiciels et dans le conseil pour aider les utilisateurs.

....

....

....

– On peut à présent régler le chauffage à distance par téléphone.

....

....

– Les ordinateurs sont souvent attaqués par des virus qui menacent de détruire les disques durs.

....

....

....

TESTEZ VOS CONNAISSANCES

À l'aide des questions suivantes, vérifiez votre connaissance du cours. Vous trouverez les réponses à la fin de l'exercice. Si vous n'avez pas la bonne réponse ou que vous désirez aller plus loin, vous pouvez vous reporter aux renvois vers les *background*. Certaines questions peuvent avoir plusieurs réponses.

1. A company is successful when it applies the 5 Ps of the marketing mix:

a. selling a good product ❏
b. in the right place ❏
c. at the right price ❏
d. to popular people ❏
e. with adequate promotion ❏

▶ **Background** *p. 115*

2. Efficient managers:

a. are amateurs ❏
b. don't care about their staff ❏
c. are professionals ❏

▶ **Background** *p. 115*

3. Companies become corporate citizens because:

a. they wish to put forward ethical values ❏
b. their board members are good citizens ❏
c. they want to differentiate themselves from their competitors ❏

▶ **Background** *p. 115*

4. Companies streamline their operations when:

a. their profits are high ❏
b. they make losses ❏
c. the company's share value is plummeting ❏

▶ **Background** *p. 116*

5. When companies expand abroad:

a. they must be ready to face local competition ❏
b. they can impose their products to local customers ❏
c. they must adapt to local tastes ❏

▶ **Background** *pp. 117-118*

6. Welfare policies:

a. reduce labour costs ❏
b. guarantee workers' benefits ❏
c. increase labour costs ❏

▶ **Background** *p. 124*

7. Teleworking is not developing as expected because:

a. people feel isolated at home ❏
b. people miss contacts with their colleagues ❏
c. people do not like working with the television on ❏

▶ **Background** *p. 125*

8. "Temping" is growing because:

a. it is a way for companies to reduce their labour costs ❏
b. it is a way for employees to organize their lives ❏
c. it is a way for people to work part-time ❏

▶ **Background** *p. 125*

9. The introduction of flexible working hours enables:

a. staff to be paid higher salaries ❑
b. firms to reduce their costs as they hire staff "just-in-time", according to the demand ❑
c. staff to keep jobs which , otherwise, would be relocated abroad ❑

▶ **Background** *p. 125*

10. The marketers' new consumer targets are:

a. children ❑
b. single people ❑
c. pets ❑

▶ **Background** *p. 135*

11. Smart cards are:

a. store loyalty cards ❑
b. plastic cards with information embedded in a computer chip ❑
c. used all over the world ❑

▶ **Background** *p. 134*

12. Hypermarkets are popular because:

a. they offer limited ranges of articles ❑
b. they are located in high streets where parking is easy ❑
c. they sell at low prices because they buy their supplies in bulk ❑

▶ **Background** *p. 139*

13. Department stores have adapted to new purchasing trends:

a. they have kept their old-fashioned image ❑
b. they sell upmarket brands ❑
c. they have introduced specialized "corners" ❑

▶ **Background** *p. 139*

14. The warming of Planet Earth leads to:

a. floods and droughts more often ❑
b. higher productivity in agriculture ❑
c. the development of transgenic products ❑

▶ **Background** *pp. 149-150*

15. The problems concerning our environment will be solved if:

a. government reduce taxes and recycling ❑
b. global climate conferences fail ❑
c. renewable energies are developed ❑

▶ **Background** *p. 152*

16. With Information Technology:

a. mobile phones cannot be connected on the Internet ❑
b. information on the Internet is always reliable ❑
c. computers have become user-friendly ❑

▶ **Background** *p. 152*

Réponses : 1a, b, c, e ; 2c ; 3a, c ; 4b, c ; 5a, c ; 6b, c ; 7a, b ; 8a, b ; 9b, c ; 10a, b ; 11b ; 12c ; 13b, c ; 14a ; 15c ; 16c.

1 Lire et comprendre un texte

Les épreuves d'anglais dans les sections de BTS tertiaires ont souvent pour support des articles de la presse anglo-saxonne.

À l'écrit, les référentiels prévoient un résumé (aussi appelé « contraction ») ou un compte rendu (aussi appelé « présentation ») en français ou en anglais.

À l'oral, le texte (de 250 à 400 mots) est le point de départ à un entretien de 15 à 20 minutes en anglais.

En conséquence, une part importante de votre formation a pour objet la compréhension d'articles de presse.

1 Repérer la construction d'un article

Un article est construit de la manière suivante :

- il commence par un titre ;
- le premier paragraphe comporte l'essentiel des informations, à moins que ce paragraphe ne soit un exemple, pour « accrocher le lecteur » ; dans ce cas, les informations viennent ensuite, dans le deuxième paragraphe ;
- le reste de l'article apporte des précisions, des détails et complète l'information.

2 Repérer les différents types de titres

a. Les titres généraux

MATTEL

Business Week, April 9, 2001.

Youth, Inc

The Economist, December 23, 2000.

b. Les titres explicites

Wages are £2,000 higher in the South

Metro, July 2001.

Ice records from 9th century show global warming

International Herald Tribune, July 2001.

▶▶▶

1 Lire et comprendre un texte (suite)

c. Les titres avec astuces

> **"Home Sweet Phone" Era**
>
> *International Herald Tribune*, October 18, 2000.

> **The Danes and Euroland: To Be or Not to Be**
>
> *Time*, April 2001.

3 Analyser un texte

Steelmaker In Britain to Slash Jobs

LONDON – Corus Group PLC, Britain's top steelmaker, said Friday that it planned to cut 1,210 jobs, or more than 3 per cent of its domestic work force, the second such move within a month, to reduce its exposure to the strength of the pound.

The former British Steel PLC said the cuts were in addition to 1,400 job losses announced in June and more could follow.

Glyn Wheeler, head of Corus's construction and engineering division, where the job losses were concentrated, said the pound was hurting exports into Europe despite a recent drop against the euro.

"Despite the recent fall, the sustained strength of sterling against the euro continues to cause severe competitive disadvantages for our business and our UK customers," he said.

The pound has risen 18 per cent against the euro since the single currency's introduction in 1999.

The job cuts will be in the north of England and in Scotland, wiping out 15 per cent of the work force at three plants in the regions. The union for workers at the plants called on London to commit to join the euro.

International Herald Tribune, July 15, 2000.

steel: acier
to slash: supprimer
pound/sterling: livre sterling (£)
former: précédemment
currency: monnaie
union: syndicat

a. La lecture du titre

1. Repérez les mots-clés correspondant aux questions en *Wh-* (*Who? What? When? Where? Why?*).
2. Utilisez des surligneurs de couleurs différentes pour repérer les questions en *Wh-*.
3. Pour faire ce travail, construisez un tableau comme dans l'exemple ci-dessous :

Questions en *Wh-*	Mots-clés du titre
Who?	*steelmaker*
Does what?	*slash jobs*
Where?	*in Britain*
When?	–
Why?	–

▶▶▶

4. Notez que :
- les titres sont rarement des phrases complètes. Manquent souvent les éléments syntaxiques non accentués (articles, auxiliaires, etc.) car, pour attirer le lecteur, il faut être court et percutant ;
- les mots commencent souvent par des majuscules, même si ce ne sont pas des noms propres.

Exemple dans le titre suivant : *Steelmaker In Britain to Slash Jobs* = ***a* s*teelmaker in Britain* *is going to* s*lash* j*obs.***

b. La lecture du premier paragraphe

1. Repérez les passages qui correspondent aux questions en *Wh-* (*Who? What? Where? When? Why?*).

2. Utilisez des surligneurs de la même couleur que celle utilisée pour le travail sur le titre pour chaque question en *Wh-*.

3. Pour faire ce travail, construisez un tableau comme dans l'exemple ci-dessous :

Questions en *Wh-*	Texte du premier paragraphe
Who?	*Corus Group PLC, Britain's top steelmaker*
Does what?	*said [...] it planned to cut 1,210 jobs, 3% of its [...] work force*
Where?	*[...] domestic [...]* (= *in Britain*)
When?	*Friday* (→ date de l'article = *July 2000*)
Why?	*to reduce its exposure to the strength of the pound*

Le premier paragraphe apporte des précisions sur le nom de l'entreprise (*Corus*), son statut juridique (*PLC* : S.A. cotée en bourse), sa position en Grande-Bretagne (*n° 1*), le nombre d'emplois qui vont être supprimés (*1,210*, soit 3 % des effectifs), le lieu (*domestic work force* = personnel travaillant en Grande-Bretagne).

Il donne également des réponses à d'autres questions en *Wh-* : *when?* la date de l'annonce (vendredi, c'est-à-dire en juillet 2000) et *why?* la raison de ce plan (réduire l'exposition de l'entreprise au cours élevé de la livre sterling).

c. La recherche des mots inconnus

1. Faites correspondre les réponses aux questions en *Wh-* dans le titre et dans le premier paragraphe de l'article, et déduisez le sens des mots que vous ne connaissez pas.

2. Cherchez et vérifiez le sens des mots inconnus dans le dictionnaire.

d. L'analyse du reste du texte

1. Repérez les mots-clés qui répondent aux questions en *Wh-* avec des surligneurs de la même couleur que ceux utilisés dans le travail sur le titre et le premier paragraphe.

►►►

1 Lire et comprendre un texte (suite)

2. Pour faire ce travail, reportez les informations dans un tableau comme dans l'exemple ci-dessous :

Questions en *Wh-*	Texte du reste de l'article
Who?	*former British steel PLC*
Does what?	*[...] in addition to 1,400 job losses [...] 15% of the work force (in Northern England and Scotland)*
Where?	*[...] construction and engineering division [...] in the north of England and in Scotland [...] three plants*
When?	-
Why?	*[...] the pound was hurting exports [...] causes severe competitive disadvantages for our business and our UK customers [...] 18% (rise for the pound) since the single currency's introduction in 1999.*

La suite de l'article apporte des détails et des précisions :

- Corus était à 100 % britannique, elle ne l'est plus car elle s'est associée avec un groupe néerlandais ;
- les licenciements s'ajoutent à d'autres décidés précédemment ;
- les divisions de l'entreprise concernées sont la construction et l'ingénierie ;
- les régions de Grande-Bretagne touchées sont le nord et l'Écosse avec 3 usines ;
- le cours élevé de la livre sterling pose problème aux entreprises et aux consommateurs britanniques car leurs produits sont chers et donc non compétitifs par rapport aux produits européens.

e. Les informations complémentaires dans le texte

Repérez les autres informations dans le texte qui ne répondent pas aux questions en *Wh-* :

- l'avenir *(prospects)* : *more could follow* = d'autres licenciements sont à prévoir ;
- les réactions *(reactions/consequences)* : *The union for workers at the plants called on London to commit to join the euro* = le syndicat des ouvriers des usines concernées en appelle à Londres (c'est-à-dire au gouvernement) pour qu'il s'engage à adopter l'euro.

2 Présenter un texte ou un document vidéo à l'oral

De nombreuses sections de BTS ont un document à présenter lors d'une épreuve orale. Le support est un texte inconnu (article, publicité, graphique) dont la longueur varie entre 250 et 400 mots selon la section, ou bien un document vidéo d'environ 2 minutes, extrait de journaux télévisés (*Sky News, CNN, BBC, ABC News*). Le temps de préparation est en général de 20 minutes.

1 Préparer un texte écrit

a. La lecture du texte

1. Lisez tout d'abord le texte en entier.

2. Relisez-le en y repérant les informations essentielles. Vous trouverez ces idées en répondant aux questions en *Wh-* (*Who? What? Where? When? Why?*).

3. Numérotez les paragraphes.

4. Surlignez les idées essentielles (utilisez des surligneurs de couleurs différentes).

b. L'introduction

Apprenez les formules utiles afin de ne pas faire d'erreurs dès le début :

- pour donner l'origine du document : *"This article comes from/was published in..., This document dated.../comes from..."* N'utilisez pas le mot *"extract"* (à la rigueur : *"text, passage, excerpt"*) ;

- pour rendre compte de l'idée générale en une phrase qui réponde aux questions en *Wh-* : *"It deals with..., reports on..., studies/analyses..."* N'utilisez pas *"to speak about"* mais à la rigueur *"to talk about"*.

c. Le plan

Il dépend, bien entendu, du document qui vous est soumis.

1. Commencez par exposer le problème, l'entreprise, le nouveau produit, le phénomène, etc.

2. Selon le document, orientez-vous vers un plan logique : causes et conséquences, avantages et inconvénients, réactions positives et négatives, projets, perspectives, limites, etc.

3. N'oubliez pas de conclure sur le texte.

d. Branching out

Le *branching out* est un commentaire et le prétexte d'un dialogue avec votre examinateur.

Il s'agit, le plus souvent, d'un élargissement de l'article à un contexte plus général.

Pour vous aider, utilisez les *background* des différents chapitres et faites des rapprochements avec d'autres documents travaillés en cours ou vus dans les différents médias.

▶▶▶

2 Présenter un texte ou un document vidéo à l'oral (suite)

2 Préparer un document vidéo

a. Les conditions d'examen

Vous disposez de 20 minutes de préparation en tout, visionnement compris.

Le document est, en général, proposé 3 fois, avec environ 10 minutes de battement entre le deuxième et le troisième visionnement.

L'épreuve consiste en un exposé du document et un entretien sur le thème évoqué.

b. L'écoute du document

1. Ne prenez pas de notes lors du premier visionnement. Regardez les images, les personnages, les noms cités, les chiffres inscrits et l'environnement du document. Tous ces éléments vous aideront à comprendre le message.

2. Après les deux premiers visionnements, posez-vous les questions en *Wh-* (*Who? Does what? Where? When? Why?*).

c. L'introduction

Utilisez les formules suivantes : "*This video was broadcast on...*" (nom de la chaîne TV + date), *It reports on..., studies..., shows...*"

d. Le plan

Il dépend, bien entendu, du document qui vous est soumis.

1. Commencez par exposer le problème, l'entreprise, le nouveau produit, le phénomène, etc.

2. Selon le document, orientez-vous vers un plan logique : causes et conséquences, avantages et inconvénients, réactions positives et négatives, projets, perspectives, limites, etc.

3. N'oubliez pas de conclure sur le texte.

e. Branching out

Le *branching out* est un commentaire et le prétexte d'un dialogue avec votre examinateur.

Il s'agit, le plus souvent, d'un élargissement du document à un contexte plus général.

Pour vous aider, utilisez les *background* des différents chapitres et faites des rapprochements avec d'autres documents travaillés en cours ou vus dans les différents médias.

3 Rédiger un résumé ou un compte rendu

Les référentiels des BTS tertiaires prévoient à l'écrit un résumé (aussi appelé « contraction ») ou un compte rendu (aussi appelé « présentation »), en anglais ou en français, à partir de textes en anglais ou en français.

En conséquence, il est important de lire avec beaucoup d'attention l'intitulé de l'épreuve qui vous est proposé et de bien faire la différence entre un résumé et un compte rendu.

1 Repérer la différence entre un résumé et un compte rendu

a. Le résumé

Un résumé est la réduction objective d'un document, en général au tiers.

1. Restez objectif(ve) : ne citez pas les sources, ne prenez aucun recul, mettez-vous à la place de l'auteur.
2. Suivez l'ordre chronologique du texte, sans introduction ni conclusion.

b. Le compte rendu

Un compte rendu est l'exposé construit et synthétique du contenu d'un document.

1. Faites une introduction en citant les sources (origine du document et date de publication).
2. Proposez un plan structuré, sans obligatoirement respecter la chronologie du texte.
3. Concluez, d'abord sur le texte proposé, puis avec un commentaire, un jugement appréciatif, un examen critique.

2 Repérer les idées dans le texte proposé

1. Soyez rapide et efficace.
2. Numérotez les lignes ou les paragraphes pour gagner du temps.
3. Lisez le texte une fois en entier pour repérer l'idée générale.
4. Posez-vous systématiquement les questions en Wh- (*Who? What? When? Why? Where?*).

3 Hiérarchiser les idées essentielles et secondaires

1. Allez à l'essentiel, ne retenez les exemples que lorsqu'ils sont indispensables à la compréhension du document.
2. Travaillez avec des surligneurs :
- pour un résumé : établissez la liste des informations repérées chronologiquement dans le texte ;
- pour un compte rendu : établissez aussi une liste d'informations trouvées chronologiquement dans le texte, puis construisez votre compte rendu synthétique avec introduction, plan, conclusion et *branching out*.

4 Relire

1. Posez-vous la question suivante : « Mon résumé/compte rendu est-il fidèle à l'article proposé ? »
2. Vérifiez la qualité de l'expression.
3. Pensez à indiquer le nombre de mots en fin de travail.

4 Traduire de l'anglais en français

La version qui peut vous être demandée à certains écrits est une restitution fidèle en français d'un texte écrit en anglais.

1 Lire le texte

Lisez le texte une fois en entier, même si on vous demande de ne traduire qu'un passage. Le contexte vous aidera à comprendre.

2 Repérer le passage à traduire

1. Repérez le passage à traduire avec des marques visibles.
2. Repérez les structures logiques (formes verbales, en particulier les mots de liaison, les mots composés, ou encore la ponctuation).
3. Ne négligez pas les pronoms : il faut repérer soigneusement les mots qu'ils remplacent.

3 Identifier les mots inconnus

a. L'analyse des mots inconnus en contexte

Ne vous bloquez pas sur les mots que vous ne connaissez pas. Un mot inconnu trouvera un sens dans le contexte de la phrase.

b. L'analyse de la fonction d'un mot dans une phrase

1. Posez-vous la question : « S'agit-il d'un verbe, d'un nom, d'un adverbe, d'un adjectif, etc. ? »
2. Pensez aux modifications d'orthographe :
- *y* devient *i* quand on ajoute un suffixe. Exemples : *-ed: to try* → *tried, -er: easy* → *easier, -est: happy* → *happiest* ;
- si elle suit une voyelle unique au son simple, la consonne finale est doublée avant d'ajouter le suffixe. Exemples : *-ed: to gun* → *gunned, -er: thin* → *thinner, -est: fat* → *fattest* ;
- quand le mot se termine par un *e*, on ajoute seulement le suffixe *-d* (au lieu de *-ed*), *-r* (au lieu de *-er*) et *-st* (au lieu de *-est*). Exemples : *-ed: to place* → *placed, -er: write* → *writer, -est: safe* → *safest.*
3. Pour les noms composés, isolez-les dans la phrase par des traits. Souvenez-vous qu'il faut, pour les traduire, commencer par le dernier mot et remonter vers la gauche.

c. Le travail avec le dictionnaire

1. Familiarisez-vous avec votre dictionnaire.
2. Prenez l'habitude de vérifier les différents sens d'un mot inconnu, ne vous arrêtez pas au premier sans réfléchir.

4 Rédiger la traduction

1. Produisez une traduction fidèle du texte anglais proposé.
2. Respectez le sens des phrases, sans ajout ni omission.
3. Ne « brodez » pas autour du texte, traduisez chaque mot.
4. Exprimez-vous dans un français clair : un lecteur doit comprendre votre traduction sans avoir besoin d'aller lire le texte de départ.
5. Exprimez-vous dans un français grammaticalement correct, sans fautes d'orthographe.

▶▶▶

5 Connaître les principaux procédés utilisés en version

a. L'emprunt

1. Vous pouvez ne pas traduire certains mots entrés dans la langue française (exemples : week-end, parking, sandwich, milkshake, beefsteak).

2. Mais, lorsque le terme existe en français, traduisez-le (exemples : *fast food* = restauration rapide ; *leader* = de premier plan, chef de file ; *marketing* = mercatique).

b. Le calque

Certains noms de lieux ou d'organismes sont calqués sans traduction (exemples : l'Empire State Building, le Far West).
Attention aux noms propres qui peuvent figurer sans *Mr, Mrs* ou *Ms* dans le cours de l'article : rétablissez le titre dans la traduction (*O'Connor said...* → Mr/Mrs/Ms O'Connor a déclaré...).

c. La transposition

Elle signifie que l'on change la nature grammaticale du mot à traduire.
Par exemple :
- nom ↔ verbe :
They spend too much on employees' wages → Ils dépensent trop pour rémunérer leurs employés.
- adverbe ↔ verbe :
They may be opening → Ils vont peut-être ouvrir
- adjectif ↔ nom :
A new body to regulate trade → La création d'un organisme chargé de réglementer les échanges
- verbe ↔ groupe nominal :
An economist said that... → Selon un économiste, ...
- chassé-croisé :
She ran out of the house → Elle sortit de la maison en courant.
Ce procédé est presque systématiquement utilisé pour les verbes exprimant un mouvement.

d. L'étoffement

Ce principe signifie que l'on ajoute un ou plusieurs mots par rapport au texte de départ pour exprimer le même message.
Exemple : *a record $60M* → un chiffre record de 60 millions de dollars.

6 Relire

1. Vérifiez l'exactitude de ce que vous avez écrit par rapport au texte proposé.
2. Vérifiez la correction de la langue française... et l'orthographe !

5 Rédiger un CV pour une demande de stage

Votre CV doit être dactylographié et tenir sur une seule page.

CV/CURRICULUM VITÆ

Stéphanie MARTIN (1)
15 rue La Fontaine
F-75015 PARIS
tel: 06 15 30 57 23
email: stephma@free.fr

Date of birth: 9 June 19__ (19 years old) (2)
Sex: female (3)
Nationality: French
Marital Status: single (4)

EDUCATION (5)

200_-to present	Currently attending a two-year post A-level course at (*name of school*) in (*town/city*), to become a business assistant (6). (BTS (*name*) exam to be taken in June 200_)
200_-200_	French Baccalaureate passed in June 200_ This examination is the French equivalent of British A-levels/US High School graduation. I specialized in… (7)

WORK EXPERIENCE

July 200_	Summer job as a secretary at the Paris Rue de Grenelle Crédit Français Bank. I answered the phone, wrote letters, dealt with clients' enquiries and complaints. (8)
200_-200_	Volunteer work for an old people's association where I live (at weekends).
March 1999	Two-week internship/work placement required by the school. I carried out a survey for a consumers' association. (9)

LANGUAGES

French: native speaker.
English: read, spoken, written. Fairly fluent.
Spanish/German: read, spoken, written. Good school level. (10)

ADDITIONAL INFORMATION

Computer skills: Word, Excel, Powerpoint. Clean driving licence. First Aid Diploma.

PERSONAL INTERESTS

Dancing: I have done classical dancing in a club for the last 4 years.
Football: I played in a club for 5 years, from 200_ to 200_ (11)

REFERENCES

Available on request (12)

Notes

(1) Écrire d'abord le prénom en minuscules, puis le nom de famille en majuscules.

(2) Écrire la date en toutes lettres (les Américains placent toujours le mois en premier : l'écrire en toutes lettres évite les confusions). On a le choix entre *9 June 19__/9th June 19__/June 9th 19__/June 9, 19__*. On peut également indiquer son âge : (*19* ou *19 years old*).

(3) Les prénoms imposent cette précision. *Lawrence* est, par exemple, un prénom masculin en anglais.

(4) Se limiter à *single* (célibataire) ou *married* (marié).

(5) Un étudiant (qui n'a pas beaucoup d'expérience professionnelle) débutera par la rubrique *Education*, tandis que quelqu'un qui a déjà travaillé commencera par *Work Experience*. Commencer par le plus récent et remonter dans le temps (jusqu'au Bac suffit).

(6) Préciser le BTS : Assistant de direction (*Bilingual Personal Assistant/PA*), Assistant secrétaire trilingue (*Trilingual PA*), Commerce international (*International Trade Relations*), Comptabilité Gestion (*Accountancy*), Action commerciale (*Marketing*), Force de vente (*Sales and Marketing*), PME-PMI (*Small- and Medium-Sized Firm*), Communication des entreprises (*Advertising*), Professions immobilières (*Real Estate*), etc.

(7) Préciser la section L/ES/STT/SMS et sa spécialité : *arts and languages* (L), *maths/physics/biology* (S), *economics/languages/maths/history and geography* (ES), *office practice/accountancy/business and marketing* (STT), *medical studies* (SMS), *computer studies* (IGestion).

(8) Autres emplois que l'on a pu avoir : *nanny for young children, waiter/waitress, kitchen help, maid, nurse aide, chambermaid, clerk/employee, sales assistant, supervizer/counselor in a holiday camp for children, cashier*, etc.

(9) Ou bien : *I worked as a sales assistant, as a secretary*, etc.

(10) Ne pas se surévaluer : *fluent* (excellent niveau), *fairly fluent* (très bon niveau), *good working/school level* (niveau correct), *basic notions* (niveau moyen).

(11) Expliquer l'activité pratiquée en détail. Ne pas se contenter de la citer.

(12) Fournies sur demande.

6 Rédiger une lettre de demande de stage

Une lettre de motivation à destination d'un pays anglo-saxon doit être dactylographiée. Elle doit vous différencier parmi les autres candidats. En conséquence, ne recopiez pas celle-ci telle quelle, adaptez-la, en parlant de vous, de votre expérience, de vos atouts pour ce stage.

15 rue La Fontaine
F-75015 PARIS (1)

Jane BROWN (2)
Human Resources Manager
O'CONNOR Company
150 Queen's Road
LONDON LN2 6JK

15th May 200_ (3)

Dear Ms BROWN (4)

APPLICATION FOR { INTERNSHIP (5) / WORK PLACEMENT }

I am writing to you on the recommendation of my English teacher/of Mr X who met you last year in ...

(or) I was impressed by your company's dynamism after reading an article in ..., after visiting your stand at the ... Trade Fair last year ... after seeing your web site ...

I would like to make an initial enquiry into the possibility of doing a 6-week work placement in your company.

I am a French student in the first of a two-year technical course in business studies (6). We study office practice, communication techniques and word-processing, economics, law and international trade.

A six-week work placement abroad is compulsory/very appreciated in the curriculum. I will have to present a description of the company, and the tasks I carried out at next year's oral examination.

I would be very grateful if you would be kind enough to consider my application for a work placement/an internship/from ... to... A placement in your company would be a marvellous opportunity for me, would enable me to gain experience in a foreign company and allow me to use my English for practical purposes. (7)

Should you need further information, please do not hesitate to contact me.

I look forward to hearing from you soon.

Yours sincerely,

(signature)

Stéphanie MARTIN

Enc.: 2 (8)
- 1 CV
- a list of the tasks I can carry out for you (9)

Notes

(1) L'expéditeur peut être indiqué à droite (adresse seule), ou bien à gauche (nom et adresse) dans le cas d'une lettre individuelle (et non d'une lettre d'entreprise à entreprise).

(2) Le destinataire est indiqué à gauche. Il est préférable de connaître son nom (le chercher, téléphoner dans l'entreprise).

(3) La date peut être placée entre l'expéditeur et le destinataire, à gauche, ou à droite, ou en haut à gauche. Mais jamais de précision sur le lieu avant la date, contrairement au français. Pour plus de précisions sur la date, voir note 2, p. 176.

(4) Si le nom du destinataire n'est pas connu, commencer la lettre par *Dear Sir or Madam*, ou *Dear Sirs*. La terminer alors par *Yours faithfully* en G.-B. et *Yours truly* aux États-Unis. Si le nom du destinataire est connu, commencer la lettre par *Dear Mr X, Dear Mrs Y*, ou encore, si on ne connaît pas l'état matrimonial d'une femme, par *Dear Ms Z.* Ne pas reprendre le prénom. Terminer dans ce cas par *Yours sincerely*.

(5) Stage : *work placement* en G.-B., *internship* aux États-Unis.

(6) Préciser la spécialité.

(7) Ajouter ici des réflexions personnelles, originales.

(8) *Enc.* en bas de page sert à indiquer les pièces jointes.

(9) Préciser les tâches que l'on est capable d'accomplir : *translating leaflets and brochures, designing brochures, writing reports in English/French/Spanish, classifying records/letters/files, creating/displaying statistical reports, creating/updating customers/suppliers/staff files, making internal/external enquiries, sending mailing lists, telephone answering and follow-up, welcoming/ taking charge of visitors, organising business trips abroad, preparing trade fairs/exhibitions/ commercial events, organizing meetings/conferences/seminars/ open days, registering simple account operations, following up orders, dealing with import-export files.*

Survival

7 Parler de son expérience professionnelle

Lors des épreuves orales, on peut vous demander de parler de votre expérience professionnelle et/ou de vos stages et actions professionnelles en entreprise. Il est important de savoir s'exprimer sur ce sujet.

1 Situer le stage ou les actions professionnelles

a. Le plan de votre intervention

1. Dites à quel moment vous avez effectué ce stage dans votre cursus scolaire.
2. Présentez l'entreprise avec des documents professionnels (rapport annuel, organigramme, etc.).
3. Évoquez sa taille, son secteur d'activité, son implantation, ses concurrents.
4. Dites comment vous avez trouvé le stage : avez-vous prospecté seul(e), par connaissance, avec vos professeurs, etc. ?

b. Le vocabulaire utile

action professionnelle : *professional assignment/task*
compétence : *skill*
concurrent : *competitor*
entreprise : *company*
études : *studies*
expérience professionnelle : *work experience*
faire un stage : *to do work experience/a work placement an internship*
formation : *training*
formation en alternance : *day-release vocational training*
lieu : *location*
secteur : *industry*
stage : *work placement, internship*
obligatoire : *mandatory, compulsory*

c. Les expressions utiles

My 2-year course specialized in... (office practice, communication tools, trade negociations, accountancy, marketing, commerce, business studies) includes vocational training in the same company 1 day a week and during... weeks work experience. I worked for..., a (secteur) company.
I carried out several professional assignments...

2 Faire une présentation détaillée des activités

a. Le plan de votre intervention

1. Exposez les tâches spécifiques confiées par l'entreprise.
2. Présentez vos réalisations : fichiers, factures, courriers, mailings, études, etc.
3. Citez les outils que vous avez utilisés : traitement de texte, tableur, téléphone, Internet, fax, etc.
4. Évoquez les problèmes rencontrés : relations, suivi du travail, délais, etc.

b. Le vocabulaire utile

courrier : *letters, mail*
date limite : *deadline*
étude : *survey*
facture : *invoice*
fichier : *file*
mettre à jour : *to update*

▶▶▶

relations : *human relationships*
rendez-vous : *appointment*
responsable de... : *in charge of...*
stagiaire (pour un étudiant) : *student/intern/trainee*
suivi du travail : *follow-up work*
tableau : *chart*
tableur : *spreadsheet*
tâche : *task*
traitement de texte : *word processing*

c. Les expressions utiles

I was in charge of.../I was told to...
I carried out several tasks (typing, answering the phone, sending faxes, contacting customers, making appointments, updating files...).
I learnt how to... (place orders, write invoices, answer claims, write out memos and minutes of meetings, reports, classify records, files, letters of enquiry, follow-up letters).
I learnt how to talk/smile on the telephone.

3 Analyser son expérience

a. Le bilan

1. Demandez-vous si cette expérience fut, pour vous et pour l'entreprise, un échec ou un succès, et pourquoi.
2. Évaluez vos résultats :
- sur le plan des connaissances professionnelles (acquisitions de nouvelles techniques, de nouveaux logiciels, perfectionnements) ;
- en termes de savoir-faire (autonomie, travail en équipe, participation à des réunions, respect des dates limites) ;
- en termes de relations humaines (évaluez vos réactions, votre professionnalisme, votre dynamisme, votre aptitude à faire face aux situations difficiles).

b. Le vocabulaire utile

digne de confiance : *trustworthy*
échec : *failure*
fiabilité : *reliability*
fiable : *reliable*
participer à une réunion : *to take part in a meeting*
ponctualité : *punctuality*
savoir-faire : *know-how*
succès : *success*
travail en équipe : *team-work*

c. Les expressions utiles

It was an enriching experience because...
It helped me improve my command of English/Spanish/German/Windows/technical language, etc.
I had to adapt to different ways of life.
It developed my knowledge of the professional/business world.
It encouraged me to take responsibilities.
It showed me I could be a valuable secretary/representative/salesperson/partner.
I learnt to be strict/flexible/self-confident/responsible/self-reliant/open-minded/reliable/trustworthy.

8 Trouver des informations sur les entreprises

Vous avez choisi une formation dans laquelle on étudie l'anglais commercial. En conséquence, vous serez amené(e) à parler d'entreprises sous forme d'un exposé synthétique en anglais.

Durant votre formation, vous aurez besoin d'informations pour préparer les *branching out* des textes étudiés dans cet ouvrage, et pour présenter à l'examen les entreprises où vous aurez effectué des actions professionnelles et des stages.

Dans votre vie professionnelle, vous aurez besoin, lors d'entretiens d'embauche, de connaître des informations sur les entreprises où vous souhaiterez travailler, les entreprises concurrentes et celles dont on parle dans l'actualité.

1 Où trouver des informations ?

1. Vous pouvez effectuer des recherches :
- dans des annuaires professionnels (*Kompass*, chambres de commerce) ;
- en écrivant au siège social de l'entreprise pour recevoir un rapport annuel ;
- sur Internet.

2. Vous pouvez aussi trouver des informations en lisant des articles dans la presse française ou anglophone ou en regardant des extraits de *news* à la télévision.

2 Comment axer vos recherches ?

Vous pouvez orienter vos recherches sur :
- le nom de l'entreprise (*name of the company*) ;
- son statut (*private limited or public limited company, small- or medium-sized firm, family-owned business, quoted on the Stock Exchange*) ;
- à qui elle appartient (*Who it belongs to*) ;
- l'emplacement de son siège social (*the headquarters location*) ;
- l'organigramme de l'entreprise (*the organization chart*) ;
- le nom du président (*chairman*), du directeur (*managing director*) ;
- le secteur d'activité (*industry*), la gamme de produits (*range of products*), les marques (*brands, makes*) ;
- la taille (*size*), le chiffre d'affaires (*turnover*), les salariés (*staff, employees, payroll*), les résultats (*results, profits*), le rang/la position de l'entreprise, sa part de marché (*how it ranks in the world, market share*) ;
- l'implantation géographique des usines et/ou des points de vente (*the geographical location of the plants, of the outlets/the points of sale*) ;
- les investissements à l'étranger (*investments, joint ventures, etc.*) ;
- les projets (*goals, prospects*) ;
- la philosophie de l'entreprise (*corporate citizen values, commitments and actions*).

3 Utiliser les informations pour faire un exposé oral

Le but de cette recherche est de faire un exposé, devant un groupe ou un jury. Pour cela, vous pouvez suivre le plan suivant :
- *Name of company*
- *Size, type of company, activity, turnover, profits, market share, position in the business environment*
- *Position at home and abroad*
- *Corporate identity and philosophy*
- *New directions, new products, prospects*

9 Prendre la parole en public

Les entreprises deviennent de plus en plus « globales », internationales. Vous serez donc amené(e), dans votre vie professionnelle, à prendre la parole en public en anglais, lors de réunions avec des collègues étrangers.
Voici quelques expressions pour exposer vos idées.

1 Starting the meeting

Shall we start?
Let's get down to business, shall we?
Could I have your attention, please?
What I want to discuss now is...

2 Exposing a situation

As you know...
Let me remind you that...
Our goal is to...
We mean to/intend to/plan to...
• *Enumerating: first/to begin with, then/next, besides/moreover, finally/as a conclusion*
• *Explaining: because + verb, because of + noun, as, since* (puisque), *owing to* (en raison de)
• *Explaining a consequence: so, that's why, consequently, thus, as a result*
• *Expressing a goal: in order (not) to, so as (not) to + noun, so that + verb*
Comparing and opposing: as in..., similarly, likewise, in the same way, unlike, contrary to, whereas, on the one hand/on the other hand

3 Asking others for their opinion

What do you think about...?
How do you feel about...?
Would you like to comment on...?

4 Giving one's opinion

In my view, personally, for me, to my mind
As far as I am concerned
I am convinced that...
Let me tell you...
I'll say that...
I think that...

5 Agreeing and disagreeing

I am entirely of the same opinion
I agree with you
I share your point of view
Mr X/Mrs Y/Ms Z is quite right when he/she says...
I don't agree/I disagree
I do not see the situation that way
I do not share your point of view

6 Concluding

This brings us to the conclusion that...
As a conclusion
To sum up, in short

10 Parler au téléphone

Dans votre vie professionnelle, vous serez amené(e) à avoir des contacts téléphoniques avec des anglophones. Vous devez, en conséquence, maîtriser les techniques de base d'une conversation téléphonique.

1 Answering the phone

- *ABC company, good morning. Can I help you?*	ABC, bonjour. Que puis-je faire pour vous ?
- *Who's calling? Who's speaking?*	Qui est à l'appareil ?
- *Who would you like to speak to?*	À qui désirez-vous parler ?
- *Hold on a minute/hold the line, please.*	Ne quittez pas, je vous prie.
- *Sorry to have kept you waiting.*	Désolé(e) de vous avoir fait attendre.
- *I'll put you through to him/her.*	Je vous mets en communication avec lui/elle.

2 Making a call

- *My name is...*	Je m'appelle...
- *Good morning. Could I speak to Mr X?*	Bonjour. Pourrais-je parler à M. X ?
- *Could you put me through to Mrs Y?*	Pourriez-vous me mettre en relation avec Mme Y ?
- *Could you put me through to extension 123?*	Pourriez-vous me mettre en relation avec le poste 123 ?
- *I'd like to speak to the person in charge of...*	J'aimerais parler au responsable de...

3 Problems of understanding

- *Could you repeat/speak more loudly/more slowly/spell your name?*	Pourriez-vous répéter/parler plus fort/plus lentement/épeler votre nom ?
- *I'm sorry you've got the wrong number.*	Désolé(e), vous avez fait un mauvais numéro.
- *The line is engaged/busy.*	Le poste est occupé.
- *Mr X is away/at a meeting/on the line.*	M. X est absent/en réunion/en ligne.
- *Would you like to hold on or would you rather ring back later?*	Préférez-vous patienter ou rappeler plus tard ?
- *Would you like to leave a message?*	Souhaitez-vous laisser un message ?
- *Would you like Mr X to call you back?*	Souhaitez-vous que M. X vous rappelle ?

4 Ending the call

- *Thank you for calling.*	Merci de votre appel.
- *You're welcome. Good bye!*	Je vous en prie. Au revoir !

11 Réviser les chiffres

Les chiffres sont très importants dans les articles de la presse économique.

• **De 13 à 19 :** suffixe *-teen* (*cf. a teenager*).
thirteen, fourteen, fifteen, sixteen, seventeen, eighteen, nineteen.
Attention aux modifications soulignées.

• **Les dizaines :** suffixe *-ty*.
twenty, thirty, forty, fifty, sixty, seventy, eighty, ninety.
Attention aux modifications soulignées.

• **Un trait d'union** entre les dizaines et les unités.
Exemples : 92 → *ninety-two.*
34 → *thirty-four.*
45 → *forty-five.*

• ***And*** entre les centaines et les dizaines, sauf en anglais américain.
Exemple : 112 → *one hundred and twelve.*

• **La virgule** marque les milliers (sauf dans les dates), mais elle ne se lit pas à voix haute.
Exemple : sept mille cinq cents → *seven thousand five hundred: 7,500.*

• ***hundred, thousand, million, billion***
Ces mots sont invariables quand ils forment des chiffres.
Ils ne prennent de « s » que dans des expressions indéterminées comme « des centaines », « des milliers », etc.
Exemples : *268 → two hundred and sixty-eight.*
6,543 → six thousand five hundred and forty-three.
Note : l'abréviation de *million* est *M* ou *m*, celle de *billion* est *bn*.

• **Les décimales**
En français, elles sont marquées par une virgule. En anglais, nous l'avons vu, la virgule sert à marquer les milliers, millions, etc.
En anglais, les décimales sont indiquées par un point.
Exemple : 4,5 (quatre virgule cinq) s'écrit en anglais *4.5* et s'énonce *"four point five"*.

• **Les ordinaux**
Ils servent pour la date, mais aussi pour les fractions.
Exemple : 1/5 (un cinquième) s'énonce *"one fifth"*.
Les fractions où les ordinaux ne sont pas utilisés sont 1/2 *(one half)* et 1/4 *(a/one quarter)*.
C'est toujours le deuxième mot qui prend la marque du pluriel.
Exemple : 2/3 (deux tiers) → *two-thirds.*

• **Les pourcentages** (%) se lisent *"per cent"*.

• **Le zéro**
Il est, la plupart du temps, prononcé comme la lettre « o » (numéros de téléphone, de chambre, de vol, d'immatriculation, etc.). En anglais américain, il est de plus en plus prononcé *"zero"*. Toutefois, si le nombre est inférieur à 1, le « 0 » qui se trouve avant la virgule se dit *"nought"*.
Exemple : 0,001 (zéro virgule zéro zéro un) s'écrit en anglais *0.001* et s'énonce *"nought point oh oh one"*, ou encore *"point oh oh one"*.

• **Les monnaies**
En chiffres, la devise est toujours indiquée avant (à gauche de) la somme.
Quand une somme est lue à haute voix, ou lorsqu'elle est écrite en toutes lettres, la devise vient en dernier.
Exemples :
£100 → *one hundred pounds.*
$700 → *seven hundred dollars.*
€30 → *thirty euros.*

• **Les proportions**
Les prépositions utilisées sont *in* ou *out of.*
Exemple : un sur quatre → *one in four/one out of four.*

12 Analyser des graphiques

Commenter un graphique requiert quelques compétences particulières : il faut savoir l'analyser. Il faut également apprendre le vocabulaire adéquat.

1 Repérer les informations

L'analyse d'un graphique doit prendre en compte les éléments suivants :
- le sujet du graphique (évolution des ventes, de la consommation, du chômage, du prix d'une denrée, du cours d'une action en bourse, etc.) ;
- les années concernées ;
- les unités représentées (nombre de produits vendus, prix en dollars, en euros, nombre de personnes concernées, etc.) ;
- la source : elle est en général indiquée en bas ou sur le côté du graphique.

2 Utiliser le vocabulaire spécifique

a. Les différents types de graphiques

graphique : *chart, graph*
courbe : *line graph*
camembert : *pie chart*
histogramme : *bar chart*

b. Les verbes et noms qui indiquent une augmentation (↗)

augmentation : *rise, increase, climb, jump*
augmenter : *to rise, to increase, to go up, to climb, to jump*
se redresser : *to pick up*
monter en flèche : *to soar, to skyrocket*
dépasser : *to top*

c. Les verbes et noms qui indiquent une diminution (↘)

chuter : *to fall, to drop, to decline, to decrease*
s'effondrer : *to collapse, to plummet, to nosedive*
chute : *fall, drop, decrease*
déclin : *decline*

d. La stabilité et les fluctuations

stagner : *to stagnate, to remain stable*
rester stable : *to hold steady*
atteindre un palier, se stabiliser : *to level out/off*
culminer, atteindre un pic : *to reach a peak, to climax*
atteindre un creux : *to reach a trough/a bottom low*
varier, fluctuer : *to fluctuate*
être au même niveau que : *to be level with*

e. Les prépositons

augmenter/diminuer de : *to rise/fall by*
augmenter/diminuer de... à... : *to rise/fall from... to...*
augmenter/diminuer jusqu'à : *to rise/fall to*
se monter à : *to stand at*
une augmentation/chute de : *a rise/fall of*
fluctuer entre... et... : *to fluctuate between... and...*

f. La nuance par les adjectifs ou adverbes

petit à petit : *gradual(-ly)*
brutal(ement) : *sharp(-ly)*
en flèche : *steep(-ly)*
beaucoup : *a lot, a great deal*
un petit peu : *marginal(-ly), slight(-ly)*
régulier/èrement : *regular(-ly), steady/steadily*
énormément : *considerable(-bly), substantial(-ly), dramatic(-ally)*
environ : *approximate(-ly), rough(-ly)*

▶▶▶

3 Exemple d'analyse d'un graphique

a. Le graphique

Sales of Willy teddy bears
by Playtoy company Ltd

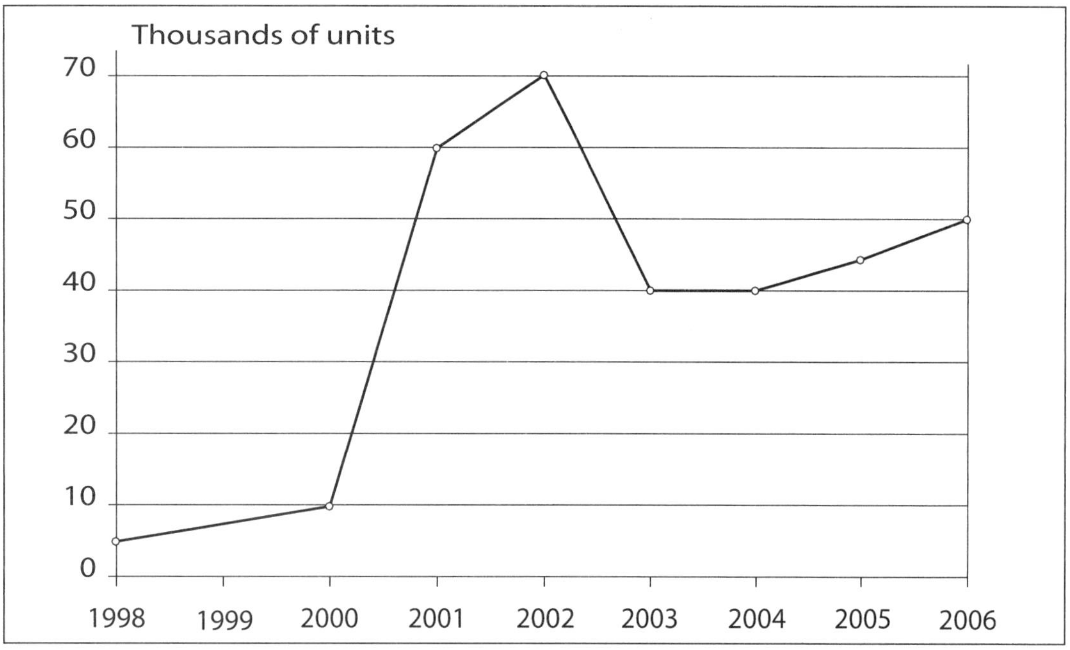

b. Le commentaire

This line graph shows the sales of Willy teddy bears by Playtoy company Ltd, between 1998 and 2006.
- In 1998, sales stood at/represented 5,000 (five thousand) units.
- Between 1998 and 2000, sales doubled. They increased regularly to reach 10,000 (ten thousand) units in 2000 (they increased to 10,000 units/they rose by 5,000 units).
- Between 2000 and 2001, sales skyrocketed/increased sharply/boomed.
- From 2001 to 2002, they soared/jumped further to reach a peak of/to climax at 70,000 (seventy thousand) units in 2002.
- Between 1998 and 2002, sales rose by 65,000 (sixty-five thousand) units/there was a rise of 65,000 units.
- However, from 2002 to 2003, sales plummeted/nosedived/collapsed/decreased dramatically by 30,000 (thirty thousand) units. They fell from 70,000 units to 40,000 (forty thousand) units.
- From 2003 to 2004, sales stagnated/levelled out at 40,000 units, business was slack.
- The market has picked up again since 2004 by 10,000 units over the past two years. The slight increase has gone on to reach 50,000 (fifty thousand) units sold in 2006.

c. Remarques

- Les verbes sont au prétérit (passé daté), sauf la fin, qui décrit une tendance qui se poursuit au moment où l'on parle (*present perfect*)
- Attention aux chiffres : il faut savoir les dire et les écrire sans erreur.
- Attention aux prépositions : *sales rose by..., sales rose to..., between... and..., from... to...*

13 The British Isles

13 The British Isles (suite)

1 Politics in Britain

– Britain/the United Kingdom (the UK) is a parliamentary monarchy made up of four regions: England, Scotland, Wales and Northern Ireland (Ulster).
Note: the adjective *British* means someone who lives in the UK.

– Britain has no constitution: it refers to statutes (Acts of Parliament) or convention.

– The monarch has symbolic functions: s/he is Head of State, of the Commonwealth, of the Church. S/he also opens or dissolves Parliament, appoints and dismisses the Prime Minister and judges.

– However, the Head of Government is the Prime Minister (PM), i.e. the leader of the majority who won a General Election (latest General Election: June 2005). S/he supervises policies and governs the country with her/his ministers.

– Parliament (in Westminster) refers to two houses:
• *the House of Commons:* 659 elected Members of Parliament (MPs) control the executive, legislate, vote taxation and decide on national policies.
Political parties: Labour, Conservative, Liberal-Democrat,
• *the House of Lords:* it has recently been transformed. The Queen and the Prime Minister still appoint Life Peers according to merit, but the number of Hereditary Peers (heads of Aristocratic families) has been cut down drastically.

2 Geography

– Britain is divided into counties (45 in England, 9 in Scotland + islands, 8 in Wales, 6 in Northern Ireland).
Many county names end in *-shire*, abbreviated with an "s": *Cambridgeshire → Cambs.*

– The Republic of Ireland (or Eire) is a completely different country.
The Republic of Ireland and Britain (plus various islands) constitute the British Isles.

3 The press in Britain

a. Quality papers

The Daily Telegraph
The Guardian
The Independent
The Times
The Financial Times

b. Popular papers

Daily Mail
The Daily Express
The Sun
The Daily Mirror
The Daily Star

c. Sunday papers

The Observer
The Sunday Times
The Independent on Sunday
The Sunday Telegraph
The News of the World

d. Weekly magazine

The Economist

14 The United States of America (The U.S.A.)

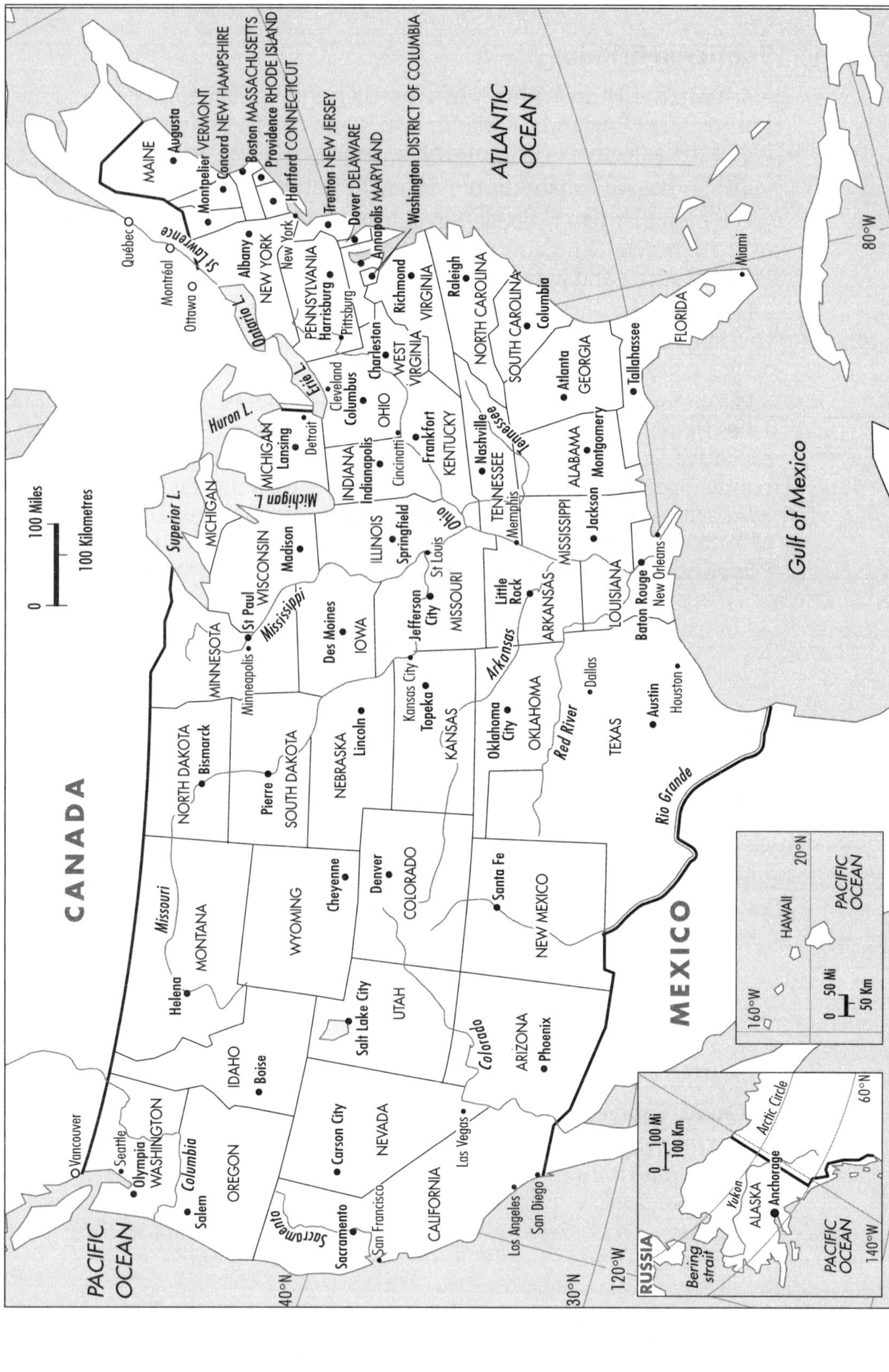

14 The United States of America (suite)

1 The US political system

The Constitution was shaped at the Convention of 1787 and signed by the 13 original states. Twenty-six constitutional amendments have been added to it. It is based on 4 principles.

a. Federalism

The USA is a confederation of 50 states.

b. Separation of powers

– Executive power is in the hands of one President (Chief Executive). S/he is elected for 4 years and can be re-elected only once. S/he is assisted by a Vice-President and a Cabinet with Secretaries for the various Departments.
– Legislative Power (Congress) is bicameral (two houses):
• *the Senate:* 100 members (2 for each state),
• *the House of Representatives:* 435 members.
– Judiciary power: the 9 Federal Judges are appointed for life by the President with the consent of the Senate.

c. Balance

The President can veto a bill, but Congress can override the veto.

d. Judicial review

The Courts can declare an act of Congress unconstitutional.
There are two major political parties:
– Democrats (symbol: donkey): they tend to be the American liberal left,
– Republicans (symbol: elephant) are the conservative right wing.

2 Geography

There are 50 states in the USA, plus the District of Columbia (where Washington, DC is located).
The states in bold are the 13 original states of the USA.

AL (Alabama)
AK (Alaska)
AZ (Arizona)
AR (Arkansas)
CA (California)
CO (Colorado)
CT (Connecticut)
DE (Delaware)
FL (Florida)
GA (Georgia)
HI (Hawaii)
ID (Idaho)
IL (Illinois)
IN (Indiana)
IA (Iowa)
KS (Kansas)
KY (Kentucky)
LA (Louisiana)
ME (Maine)
MD (Maryland)
MA (Massachussetts)
MI (Michigan)
MN (Minnesota)
MS (Mississippi)
MO (Missouri)
MT (Montana)
NE (Nebraska)
NV (Nevada)
NH (New Hampshire)
NJ (New Jersey)
NM (New Mexico)
NY (New York)
NC (North Carolina)
ND (North Dakota)
OH (Ohio)
OK (Oklahoma)
OR (Oregon)
PA (Pennsylvania)
RI (Rhode Island)
SC (South Carolina)
SD (South Dakota)
TN (Tennessee)
TX (Texas)
UT (Utah)
VT (Vermont)
VA (Virginia)
WA (Washington)
WV (West Virginia)
WI (Wisconsin)
WY (Wyoming)

3 The American press

There are hundreds of papers. The most famous dailies are *Washington Post, New York Times, USA Today, International Herald Tribune* (for American expatriates). The most famous magazines are *Time, Newsweek, Business Week* and *Fortune*.

15 The European Union

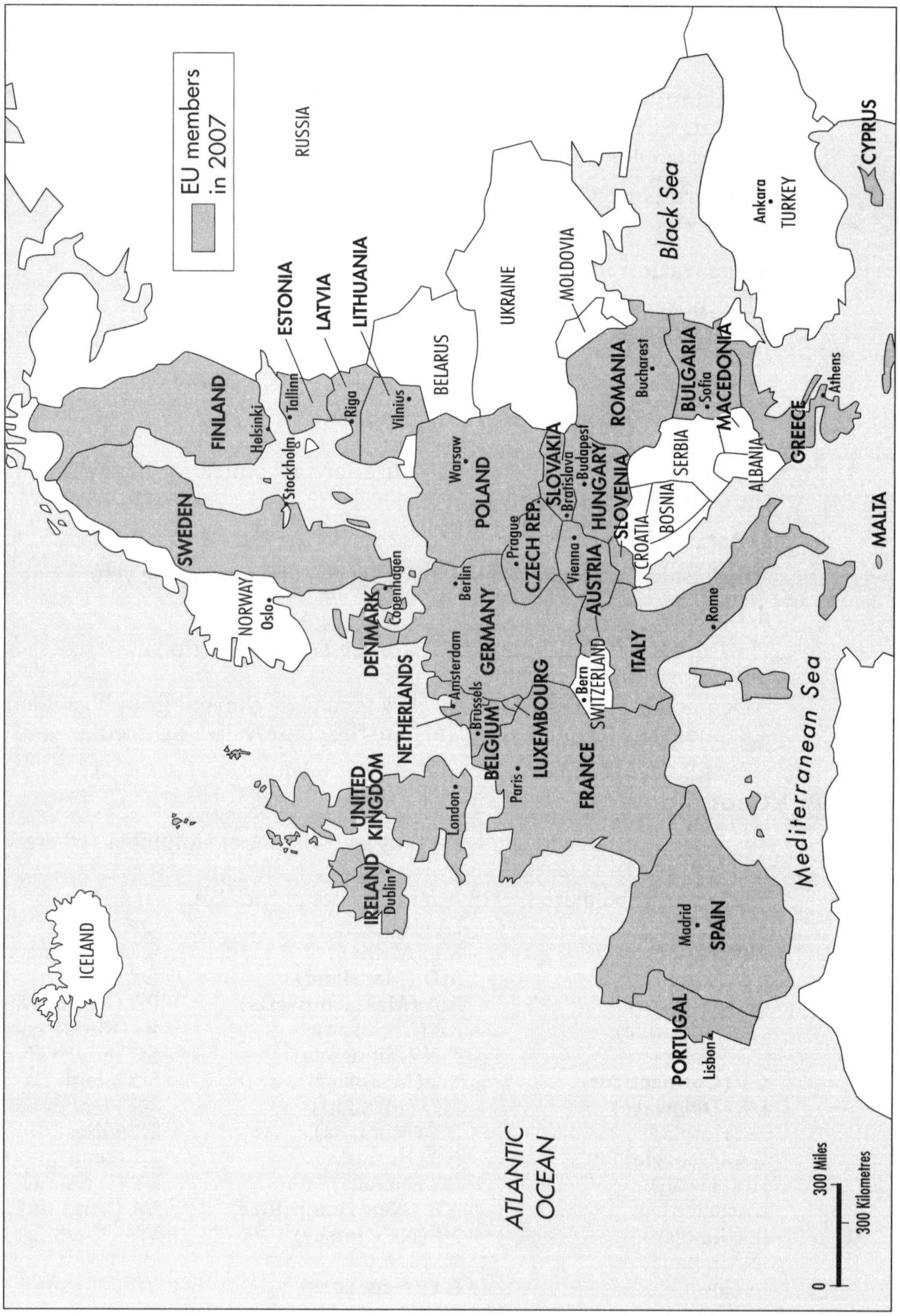

Les nationalités

Attention : en français, seuls les noms de nationalité prennent une majuscule, les adjectifs n'en prennent pas.
Exemples : C'est un **A**utrichien. Je n'aime par le vin **a**llemand.

En revanche, en anglais, il y a toujours une majuscule.
Exemples : *I think he is a* ***P****ole. I like* ***E****nglish food.*

Country	Capital	Official lang.	People: sing. a/an...	People: plural the...
Austria	Vienna	German	Austrian	Austrians
Belgium	Brussels	French/Dutch/ German	Belgian	Belgians
Britain/ the U.K.	London	English	Briton	Britons/British
Bulgaria	Sofia	Bulgarian	Bulgarian	Bulgarians
the Czech Republic	Prague	Czech	Czech	Czechs
Denmark	Copenhagen	Danish	Dane	Danes
Estonia	Tallinn	Estonian	Estonian	Estonians
Finland	Helsinki	Finnish	Finn	Finns
France	Paris	French	Frenchman	French
Germany	Berlin	German	German	Germans
Greece	Athens	Greek	Greek	Greeks
Hungary	Budapest	Hungarian	Hungarian	Hungarians
Ireland	Dublin	English/Irish	Irishman	Irish
Italy	Rome	Italian	Italian	Italians
Latvia	Riga	Latvian	Latvian	Latvians
Lithuania	Vilnius	Lithuanian	Lithuanian	Lithuanians
Luxembourg	Luxembourg	French/German	Luxembourger	Luxembourgers
the Netherlands	Amsterdam	Dutch	Dutchman	Dutch
Poland	Warsaw	Polish	Pole	Poles
Portugal	Lisbon	Portuguese	Portuguese	Portuguese
Ro(/u/ou)mania	Bucharest	Rumanian	Romanian	Romanians
Slovenia	Ljubljana	Slovene	Slovene	Slovenes
Spain	Madrid	Spanish	Spaniard	Spanish
Sweden	Stockholm	Swedish	Swede	Swedes

16 Asia

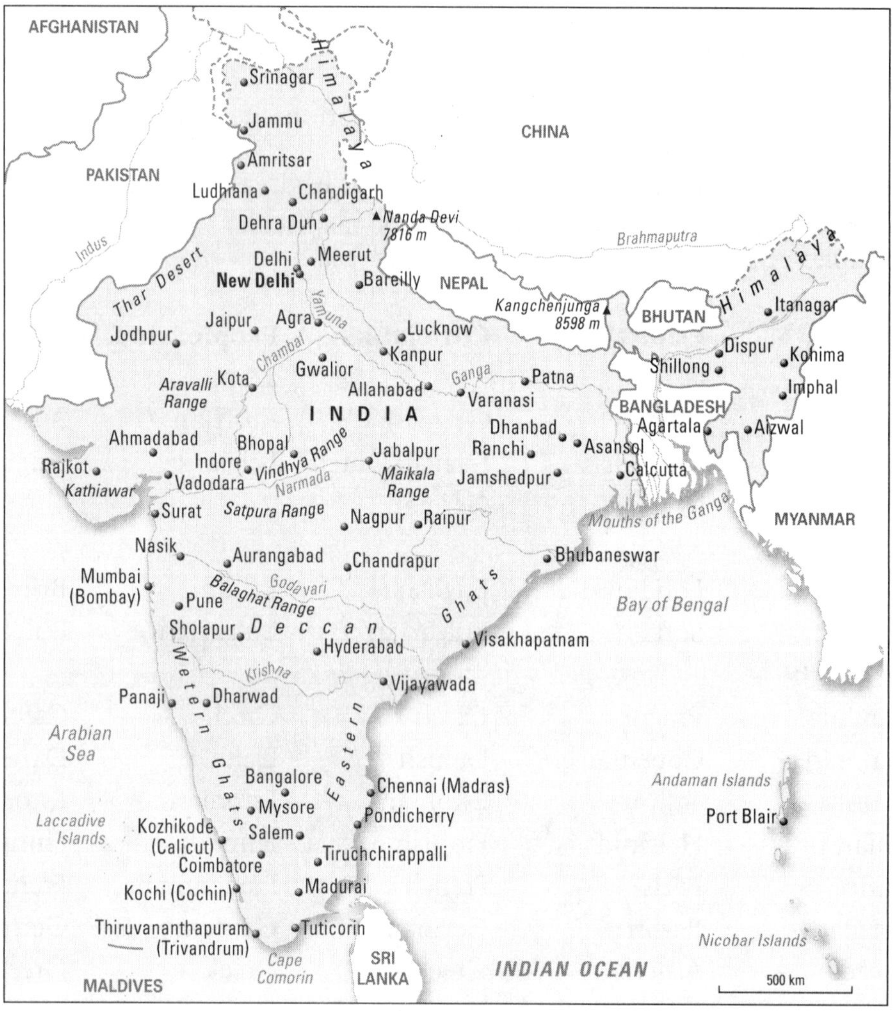

N° d'éditeur : 10137806 - CGI - Dépôt légal : Mars 2007
Achevé d'imprimer en France sur les presses de Jouve, Paris - N° 424802P